Preeti Gill is an independent editor and literary agent. As a commissioning editor and rights manager, she has more than twenty years of experience in the publishing industry. In her new role as literary agent she represents more than thirty well-known, critically acclaimed writers of fiction and creative non-fiction. Her special focus is on translations from Indian languages as well as writings from India's Northeast. She has travelled extensively in the Northeast and written on issues of conflict and women in the region.

Her books include an edited volume of essays, *The Peripheral Centre: Voices from India's Northeast*; *Bearing Witness: A Report on the Impact of Conflict on Women in Nagaland and Assam* (co-edited with Sanjoy Hazarika), and *Shadow Lives: Widowhood in India* (co-edited with Uma Chakravarty). She has edited (along with Samrat) *Insider/Outsider: Belonging and Unbelonging in Northeast India*. She is now working on an anthology of non-fiction writings on Punjab.

She has worked on a number of documentaries as scriptwriter and researcher, including *Rambuai: Mizoram's 'Trouble' Years* which she has co-produced with Sanjoy Hazarika.

Preeti Gill is the founder of Majha House, a literary and cultural centre in the city of Amritsar.

SHE STOOPS TO KILL

STORIES OF CRIME AND PASSION

Paro Anand • Venita Coelho • Uddipana Goswami
Manjula Padmanabhan • Janice Pariat
Mitra Phukan • Pratyaksha • Bulbul Sharma

Edited by PREETI GILL

SPEAKING
TIGER

SPEAKING TIGER PUBLISHING PVT. LTD
4381/4, Ansari Road, Daryaganj
New Delhi 110002

First published in paperback by Speaking Tiger 2019

Anthology copyright © Speaking Tiger 2019
Stories copyright © Individual contributors 2019

ISBN: 978-93-88874-84-7
eISBN: 978-93-88874-83-0

10 9 8 7 6 5 4 3 2 1

Typeset in Sabon LT Std by SÜRYA, New Delhi

*This book was born at the Guwahati airport
while waiting for a delayed flight.
Thank you, Sambha Lamaar, for bringing
Preeti Gill and Paro Anand together at Shillong.
You didn't know there was a book being conceived.
Hope you enjoy it, wherever you are...*

CONTENTS

INTRODUCTION

Sitting at Guwahati Airport with a bunch of fellow festival participants, waiting to catch the flight back to Delhi one December afternoon, the talk turned to murder. And as we talked about the many gory stories that colour the pages of our daily newspapers red, we tried to recall some really good Indian crime fiction that we'd read. So, as Paro Anand, partner-in-crime-anthology and contributor to this one, and I talked, it struck me that putting together an anthology of murder stories written by women might be quite an intriguing idea. The story I heard from Paro herself (written, she said with a wicked glint, as an outpouring of frustrated anger) convinced me that I'd like to 'confine' the murder to the domestic sphere and that each writer could kill off a spouse, partner, sibling, child, spurned lover, jilted paramour, what-have-you. Most of us have, perhaps, at some point in our lives, had the urge to kill (entire families killed off sometimes for a completely irrational, absolutely random reason) and so I thought, here is my chance to delve into the minds of these 'chosen' eight women—perhaps they would reveal what might actually drive them to (imagine) murder. The writers I chose for this anthology don't usually write about crime, and much less murder, but once they decided to take this on I was absolutely stunned by the variety, the enthusiasm, the imaginative detail and also the macabre bloodiness of their stories. All of them have enjoyed their foray into the dark side and some are convinced that they want to take on this genre and write a collection of such fiction or even perhaps a novel.

The human appetite for mystery, murder and mayhem cannot be doubted and from that very first Biblical story of Cain and Abel, murder and crime, and the whys and wherefores of it, have continued to fascinate us. Reading crime fiction began early and it is something I've continued to enjoy over the years. Many of the 'classics' that were recommended reading at school had at the heart of them dark, deep mysteries that caught you and pulled you into their secret worlds and whetted your appetite for more. Charles Dickens (*Bleak House*), Wilke Collins (*The Woman in White*) and then from those exalted spheres to 'popular' crime fiction written by Agatha Christie, Arthur Conan Doyle, Dorothy L Sayers, Ruth Rendell, Sara Paretsky and my own all-time favourite, P D James.

Crime writing, thrillers and mysteries could easily be thought of as genres written by and for men, probably because they are so violent. But, whether it is a Stephen King or James Patterson that flies off shelves at airports or corner bookstores, what some research studies have shown is that female readers are more drawn to crime fiction than men. And even though James Patterson might be the one getting seventeen book deals and millions in advances, some of the best writers of crime are women. Older writers like Agatha Christie and Dorothy Sayers continue to have loyal followers but the new, younger breed of women crime writers have found that the dark, deep well of the human mind is well worth gazing into to reveal the terrible angst and insecurities it hides. The books that they write are light on gunplay and heavy on emotional violence. Perhaps their kind of storytelling is a better fit for today's cynical times. Death in their novels is often chillingly casual and unnervingly intimate. As one critic says, 'Most of them kill you from the inside out.' The awareness of that inside-out sort of violence sets the women writers apart for they can be found burrowing into the enigmas of identity and the killing stresses of everyday life.

What is it that draws readers to crime fiction? From the early novels from Western shores to the most recent desi crime, the draw for me is in the detail, the building up of the locales and landscapes, be it the ugly underbelly of a sprawling metropolis or the smooth beauty of a beautifully appointed sitting room. The 'wrong place' can be suburbia, or social media, a high school or even an intensely private space like the marriage bed. The darkness is as much in the space as in the writer's head and what she writes. The spectacular success of *Gone Girl* by Gillian Flynn and *Girl on the Train* by Paula Hawkins brought murder and mayhem into the intimate space of the family and familial relationships. As Laura Miller says in *Salon*, 'Their prose ranges from the matter-of-fact to the intoxicating and the battlefields they depict are not the sleazy nightclubs, back alleys, diners and shabby offices of the archetypal PI novel but a far more intimate and treacherous terrain, family, marriage, friendship.'

Most male writers use the trope of the larger than life hero, a super sleuth whose mental agility, intelligence and meticulous, orderly, logical thinking and moral incorruptibility (even if they are often borderline alcoholics or chain smokers or chronically depressed) is in strong contrast to the almost total disorder of their personal lives and physical appearance. Women are more nuanced in their writing, I think. Perhaps violence or the implied threat of it is very real to them, its casualness in their daily life is so much a given that perhaps they feel it more intensely and this emerges in their writing.

Is this true of women crime writers closer home? With sensational murders bloodying the news pages and TV channels each day, surely there is enough meat available to fire the imagination and today we have a whole gang of women like Madhulika Liddle, Kalpana Swaminathan, Swati Kaushal, Madhumita Bhattacharyya among others striding shoulder to shoulder with Ashok Banker, Tarquin Hall, Zac O' Yeah, Ravi Subramanian, Vish Dhamija, Ankush Saikia and Amitabh Pandey. But certainly there is space for more.

Talking about the appeal of the genre, Zac says, 'Crime novels are like therapy; crime novels tell you about how to survive in the big bad city with its everyday threats and traps.'

According to Zac, the Indian detective lives within the social system and the family, he or she is not typically a loner like their counterparts in the West. There are cultural aspects that make the Indian crime novel or short story different and in many ways the stories in this anthology capture that difference, that 'specialness'. The eight women writers whose stories form part of this collection have created some memorable characters and locales while embedding their stories deep within the social system, the cultural complexity that is India. Each one brings to the telling her own peculiar talent, her own brand and persona, her own particular genius. They bring us strong feisty characters, a woman detective, a vigilante hijra, a widow with murderous intent who refuses to be a victim, and a sense of place and atmosphere that is stunning and unique.

Paro Anand, this year's winner of the Sahitya Akademi's Bal Puruskar, whose story 'And Then He Said' is the finale of the anthology, has written eighteen books for children and young adults including short stories and fairytales, novellas and plays. She is a wonderful performance storyteller—seeing her in action is a treat—and she has also worked with children impacted by violence in Kashmir and uses literature for holistic development. An unlikely candidate if there ever was one to do a murder story and yet here we have her writing of infidelity, of a dark lust and its terrible consequences.

Bulbul Sharma fans will find in 'Murder in the Wedding Season' her signature charming descriptions of small towns and close-knit families full of whimsical aunts and uncles (here one arrives for a wedding, catheter in tow!), each cleverly drawn with quick deft strokes. Her fifty-five-year-old widow who has erased her life, her carefree youth, bit by bit to blend in with the family is a true-to-life creation as is the story that unfolds within the sprawling old house where dark secrets are hidden only to come tumbling out in the bright light of day. Bulbul is a wonderful storyteller and an artist—she has a number of short story collections and a novel to her credit. She has written for children and she teaches art and writing to children with special needs. I have been completely enchanted with her funny, exuberant, lively anecdotes on many an occasion.

Venita Coelho's superb story, 'Sister', is perhaps the most grisly, the most graphic in its description of death. The smell of blood, the coagulating, slippery, sticky mass of it, the ritualistic killing, the darkness of the human heart, the everyday commonplace ugliness of it all are brilliantly done. Venita has written screenplays and television stories, ghost stories and novels and is an artist as well. Her sleuth, the hijra, Sister, huge, giant-like with a gentle voice and a kind heart is a fantastic creation and deserves to have a novel dedicated to her exploits.

Mitra Phukan is a classical vocalist and a writer who lives in Guwahati. She has used both of these to create a story, 'Poison in the Paan', which is funny, tongue-in-cheek, strongly feminist with a woman private detective who solves the murder of a singing diva that is as flamboyant as it is public. Mitra is a well-respected writer, part of the North East Writers Network, a warm wonderful friend who writes a successful column for the *Assam Tribune* newspaper called 'All Things Considered', where she often talks of the daily dilemmas of our lives and discusses in a chatty, informal way some of the deepest and most distressing issues that have engulfed our landscapes, both interior and exterior.

Janice Pariat's 'The Nurse' is a nuanced story about love and longing and dependency that ends calamitously. Her writing is like a rare gentle song, her images beautiful and delicate. Her first collection of short stories all set in her native Meghalaya won her the Sahitya Akademi Award for Best First Book and since then her writing has grown and travelled to other distant territories just as eloquently and effectively.

Writer, cartoonist and playwright Manjula Padmanabhan's story 'The Serial Killer' looks into the crazed mind of a killer, an ordinary innocuous enough young man who looks like everyone else except in his head. And she says in her collection of short stories, *Three Virgins and Other Stories*, all too often the characters and stories she writes arrive at her desk as 'rude unsightly wretches'! Her writing is dark, edgy, and fills you with a sense of unease and disquiet and this story is no different.

Uddipana Goswami's 'Beloved of Flowers' is a take on the well-known, haunting story of young Tejimola and the abuse she suffers at the hands of her stepmother, and how each time she rises phoenix-like from a violent death. It is a story of survival and strength despite the horror and bloody torture that infuse the original Asomiya story. Using that as her takeoff point Uddipana adds subtle layers to the story, carefully building up the horror to come.

Pratyaksha is a skilled storyteller, poet and painter with some six books to her credit in Hindi and English. In 'Ginny Kalra, I Loved You', she explores a murder in a Matunga flat giving us at least three suspects and then springing an unexpected twist in the best short story tradition. She uses unusual sentence formations in her writing and leaves a great deal to the imagination of the reader. Her sort of stream of consciousness style and the staccato beat of her sentence structure work well in this story.

This is, I think, the first collection of its kind in India and I'd like to say a grateful thank you to all the eight contributors for agreeing to be part of this venture and to Speaking Tiger (whose list I admire tremendously) and Ravi for sharing my enthusiasm and getting it out there.

New Delhi   Preeti Gill
May 2018

POISON IN THE PAAN

Mitra Phukan

The audience, every last man and woman, was engrossed in the recital. All eyes were on the stage. Heads were nodding in appreciation, hands and feet were beating in time to the rhythm. Every now and again, a simultaneous 'wah, wah' would escape their lips, more like a prayer than an exclamation. 'Kya baat!' somebody would breathe as the singer would execute a particularly intricate swoop, from one note to another.

Prabeena looked sideways at Himangshu. He was gazing raptly at Shraddha Devi, she of the luscious curves, quite apparent even through the folds of her magenta and parrot green Benarasi sari. Her kohl-lined eyes, glistening mouth and ample bosom, which, at the moment, was heaving mesmerizingly, synchronized beautifully with the taans and murkis that she executed. But Prabeena didn't mind. She knew that it was the aural beauty all around them Himangshu was so immersed in. He probably didn't even notice the singer's physical charms. Whereas she, Prabeena herself, was very much attuned to the visual. She had to be, in her profession.

But I shouldn't be looking around like this, she admonished herself. I paid vast sums of money to get these second row seats. Of course it's all worth it to see Himangshu enjoying himself so much. Now if only I could do the same...Shraddha Devi was, after all, one of the topmost exponents of her gharana, perhaps *the* topmost exponent of thumris and dadras. It had been difficult to get tickets, for she performed in her home town only rarely, but she had managed it.

Balamwa Pardesiya, Mora, Shraddha Devi was crooning. Certainly it sounded very nice, and Prabeena hoped that the Balamwa, the Beloved who had gone off leaving her alone, would return soon. Prabeena couldn't quite bring herself to say 'wah, wah' though.

She had to admit, however, that the whole ensemble had taken a great deal of trouble to present a picture of visual attractiveness, too. Shraddha Devi, with her shimmering clothes, glittering jewellery and flashing nose pin was very much at the centre, the focus to which the eye of the audience would inevitably be drawn. There were two mikes before her, strategically placed so that the radiance of her face would not be blocked. Before her, an intricately worked silver casket contained, she supposed, the mandatory paan which so many traditional musicians still consumed, ignoring all health warnings. A tumbler of water, from which she sipped occasionally. To her side, a large handbag, from which she had, just a while ago, taken out a book containing the lyrics of the thumri that she was now singing.

Given the visual brilliance of the star performer, the others paled into insignificance on that stage despite their sartorial efforts. Prabeena's gaze travelled from one to the other. They were all wearing colour-coordinated outfits, she realized. Sukumar Bose was tossing his head around even as his hands beat out a complicated laggi on the tablas. His whirling curls were as dramatic as his magenta kurta. Iqbal Khan on the sarangi had white hair which shone mutedly under the lights, but his green kurta was incandescent in its brightness. Rishabh Das on the harmonium was in a splendid kurta, cream but with magenta and green stripes.

Behind the dazzle of the front row were the two taanpura players. Young women, they too were dressed in the same colours of magenta and green, one in a sari, the other in a churidar kurta. They leaned forward at their Guru's command on occasion, to provide vocal support, while Shraddha Devi sipped on water, or smiled at the audience, or adjusted the folds of her sari across her ample chest. Both the students, Prabeena thought, were quite good. But they were hardly noticed, even though they carried out the vital task of playing the two taanpuras, the drone instruments without which the whole concert would be a discordant mess.

The hall was filled with connoisseurs, including Himangshu. She was the exception. She had almost sent him off alone, for if the truth be told, music was not her forte. But this was his birthday, and this her gift to him. She wanted to be near him this evening, away from the usual demands of her life. And sitting through these hours was a small price to pay for the delight on his face when she had told him that they would be going to Shraddha Devi's concert on his birthday. 'You're coming too, aren't you?' he had asked, and she had been glad to assure him that yes, she would drop everything to be near him throughout that evening, even though they both knew that this was not her scene at all.

On the stage, Shraddha Devi looked back and nodded to the student on the left. This was a signal that she was to continue, while Shraddha herself took a break. As the girl, no, Prabeena realized, the woman, began to sing, Shraddha smiled at the audience, then, took a sip of water. She leaned forward and, ignoring the efforts of the student behind her, said, 'So, Choudhury Sahib, you are liking this recital?'

The chief guest, Ranjit Choudhury, sitting in the front row, raised his hand in response. Prabeena, sitting diagonally behind him, noticed his smile, his strong profile, his greying head of hair. Shraddha had been addressing him off and on throughout the recital, but it seemed to Prabeena that her body language was getting more intimate, more coquettish. It was as though she was oblivious to the rest of them, sitting in the auditorium. In Shraddha Devi's mind, this was a baithak, and Choudhury, an honoured client. It was her duty to seduce him, through the bewitchery of her music, her beauty, her smiles, her talk.

The woman at the back, the student, continued to sing, though nobody was paying any attention to her. Surely this was bad manners on the part of the Guru, thought Prabeena. But the student, a thin woman with sharp features, continued, oblivious to the fact that the audience's attention was now focussed on the little byplay between the man and the artiste. Even Himangshu, dear man, seemed a little distracted. The other student, Prabeena noticed, was a beauty. Her Guru wasn't giving her much of a chance to put in her bit, though. She seemed not to mind, serenely continuing to play the taanpura, looking occasionally at the audience.

Though the student was in full flow, Shraddha cut her off midway now, to sing

Kaisey katey din ratiya, Balam bin,
Neend na aiye more ratiya, Balam bin

How can I get through this day, this night,
Without my beloved, sleep eludes me at night,
Without my beloved.

Her voice was silver, gold and honey, warm and tender, enticing, seductive. It was, thought Prabeena dispassionately, a bedroom voice. Was it just that she was singing these almost-erotic songs, or was her temperament like that, too? In any case, she had now abandoned all pretence of singing to the audience, and was focussing solely on Choudhury. Her smiles, her glances, her body language, were all aimed at him.

'Enjoying it?' asked Himangshu.

'More than you can imagine,' Prabeena replied. 'She's quite something, isn't she? And I don't mean musically, you know.'

'I know what you mean,' said Himangshu. 'She's... there's something not quite...I don't know how to put it.'

'She's seducing that man right under our noses,' said Prabeena helpfully. Their voices were low whispers. 'And getting away with it just because she's a famous singer. Yes, I'm enjoying this!'

Ranjit Choudhury, too, seemed to be rather enjoying the singer's attentions. Going by what she could see of his profile, he was nodding and smiling, though in a controlled and somewhat distracted manner, as befitted, she supposed, the measured dignity required of a chief guest.

Shraddha took a sip from the glass in front of her. Nose pin flashing, she gestured to the student to fill in the gap with her music. Obediently, the woman at the back leaned forward again, and began to sing. She seemed not to mind the snub that her Guru had given her earlier. Or maybe, thought Prabeena, if you were a student, you couldn't afford to be sensitive to a Guru's snubs, not while onstage, anyway. Prabeena realized she was smiling as she watched Shraddha Devi adjust her pallu once again, and then stroke back a tendril that was wisping enticingly down the side of her face.

Once more, a sip of water. Sukumar Bose and Iqbal Khan were smiling at each other, as they played along with the student, enjoying their turn. Shraddha Devi was now delicately opening the silver casket before her. She took out something fresh and green, and popped it into her mouth. Tucking the wad of paan to one side of her mouth, she continued her song, slicing into her student's singing without bothering about interrupting her at all.

'Come, Choudhury Sahib, this is for you,' she said. Smiling, she began a taan, a silvery succession of notes that climbed up the scale, like an eagle soaring into the blue sky above. Her hand, expressive as her voice, drew arcs that spiralled up, echoing the music.

But.

The unthinkable. Halfway up that taan, Shraddha Devi began to cough. Onstage, all eyes swivelled towards her. This was something that should not happen even to a beginner. How could…

The hall full of people sat up, all of them aware, suddenly, of something gone awry. A top thumri singer, her taan cut off mid-flow by a cough! Indeed, it was getting worse by the second. The hand that was executing visual music changed course and clutched at her throat instead. Her face was now flushed, contorted. As they watched, a look…of fear? Panic?… suffused it. Her eyes watered, and began to pop out. A horrible choking sound came from her, the total antithesis of the music of just a few seconds before, as, before their very eyes, she keeled over sideways. She was gasping for breath now, choking and sputtering. The musicians, on auto mode, kept playing, even as they looked at her with increasing horror. The audience had not yet grasped what was happening, as they stared, astonished, at the drama before them.

Shraddha Devi hit the durrie-covered floor of the stage with an audible thump. Froth bubbled from her mouth. Her hands flailed about, her body jerked in spasms, knocking over the microphone stand, which thudded down in a huge explosion of sound. The three men onstage kept playing, even though the song was gone. Just like a chicken which kept running around the yard even after its head was cut off.

It was a few seconds before Shraddha Devi's body stilled. The awful sounds from her throat stopped. The women behind, and the men in the front, finally laid down their instruments, not taking their eyes off the still body of Shraddha. In the auditorium, too, there was silence, except for somebody saying 'Oh my God'. Nobody moved.

Swiftly, from her aisle seat, Prabeena got up and strode to the stage, climbing the steps to the side. Without glancing at the tableau onstage, she went to the wings. Pushing aside the people who were staring at the fallen woman, she said urgently, 'Who's in charge of drawing the curtains? Quick...'

A young man came forward. He pushed a button on a console. Slowly, the maroon velvet drapes drew shut. Prabeena looked at the man behind a mike, and commanded, 'Make an announcement. Quick. Nobody is to leave their seats. Say it, immediately.'

Shifting his staring gaze to Prabeena, the MC

began to speak, in automatic mode. 'A...an accident. So sorry for this. Please remain where you are. Remain seated, please.'

'Who's in charge here?' asked Prabeena, looking around. 'The organizers, where are they? Oh, okay,' she went towards the man with the gamosa and rosette on his chest. 'Have all the doors closed, make sure nobody goes out.'

The man goggled at her.

'Do it,' she said, slowly and distinctly. Without waiting for a reply, she went to the stage now curtained off from the auditorium, and straight to Shraddha Devi's still form. Kneeling, she felt for the carotid, the pulse. Nothing. As she had expected.

Without taking her eyes off the supine form of the dead woman, Prabeena took out her cell. The person at the other end took the call immediately. The people on stage shifted their dazed gazes to her.

'Saraswati Auditorium,' she was saying briskly. 'Yes, a death. Can't say yet, no, whether it's an accident or...yes, I've had all the doors closed, nobody can go out. Yes, I'll be here.'

There were footsteps behind her. Himangshu.

'It was meant to be a good evening,' she said contritely. 'Art, Beauty, all of that. Not this at all. And now your birthday treat is spoiled.'

He came and stood near her. He didn't need to say anything, for her to know that he felt the same way as she did. Shocked. And if this was not an accident, but something else, then, horrified. And angry that somebody should have dared to stage a murder like this, right in front of everybody's eyes. Hundreds of witnesses. And yet nobody to whom one could point the finger of accusation.

Not yet, anyway, thought Prabeena, grimly.

~

Well past midnight.

The stage had been cleared, the police and forensic people had come, done their work, and left. Chalk lines marked the place where Shraddha Devi had fallen, but the body itself had been encased in plastic and taken away. Notes had been made, questions asked, people detained, people allowed to leave.

Superintendent of Police Jayanta Barua looked up at Prabeena, and sighed. 'Well, there we are then.' His gaze travelled over the familiar face and body, but he kept both voice and gaze neutral. 'Thank you for the prompt action. That helped a lot, of course.'

Prabeena shrugged. 'More reflex action than anything else. Comes from being a private detective for all these years.' She glanced at Himangshu, who was standing and looking haggardly at the chalk lines on the floor. 'If you don't need me, maybe we can go home now? I'm always at your service, of course.'

The policeman smiled at the nuance in Prabeena's voice. He lowered his own, and said, 'Why don't you hang around, we can have a bite somewhere. If you like, I can have your friend sent home in a police vehicle.'

Prabeena raised her eyebrows, and said firmly. 'My partner. We live together, remember? He's the reason we got divorced, you and I.'

'Yes, yes, of course.' Jayanta Barua said. 'Okay, go. And, umm...thanks. It's made us look good, the police force, for once. The TV channels are going on about how quickly the police arrived on the scene.'

'It's a high profile case, hope it can be cracked soon,' said Prabeena. 'So much drama. And then the lady herself, such a well-known artiste, one of India's finest.'

'Prabs, do me another favour?' said Jayanta. 'I'll be meeting the people who were on stage, and in the green room again in a couple of days. In my office. I'll be talking to them in more detail. Come over, be around, give me your impressions?' He looked at her short cropped hair, her trim litheness, but added, neutrally, 'Please? Professionally, of course?'

She smiled. 'Sure. I was hoping you'd let me in on this case, unofficially, in some way...It's intriguing, isn't it?'

Back in the car, with Himangshu driving, she thought back to the last year. Theirs had been an amicable divorce, of course. Jayanta was too civilized to make a scene about it. She knew that he had not quite understood why she, his friend of so many years, and wife of five, should feel this way about this studious academic and poet. Oh yes, he had tried to persuade her to give their marriage some more time, time to get on an even keel again, but she had just smiled and shaken her head.

Jayanta was a friend, a very good friend indeed. But they were probably too much alike. Whereas...she glanced sideways at Himangshu...with this man, there was the luminous light of poetry, the feeling that yes, there was beauty beyond the mundane, beyond the ugliness of crime, and unnatural deaths. And *murder*. There was something beyond the grime in which they both, husband and wife, Jayanta and Prabeena, were dealing with, as part of their jobs. And this man, this quiet academic with whom she had fallen hopelessly, unexpectedly in love, knew the way to that other world. He was the one who would lead her there. Over the years, Jayanta and she had collaborated on several cases, unofficially, of course. He was a brilliant, incorruptible police officer who had got into the civil services at the first shot. And she, an equally brilliant private investigator, much in demand professionally. But Jayanta had relied on her sharpness for inputs. And his colleagues, the people of his department, too, had come to respect her skills, and had even requested her to sit in on their meetings.

As they pulled up in front of the university quarters that was their home, Prabeena was glad that they still remained very good friends, she and Jayanta. And that their professional relationship, too, had remained as before.

~

Ten in the morning, two days later. The papers that day were full of pictures of Shraddha Devi, and reports about her funeral the previous day. The obituaries were long and fulsome.

Jayanta was not alone when Prabeena entered his office. Several other men and women, all, like Jayanta himself, in police uniform, were grouped around the room.

They all turned to look at Prabeena as she entered. Greetings were murmured. A chair was pulled up near the large desk for her.

'The first of the witnesses is just due in,' said Jayanta. He turned to the police people around him, and added, 'I've requested Prabeena to sit in on this. Ah...professionally, of course. As you know, she was right there when it happened. Her insights will be valuable, I thought, given her long experience as a highly regarded private investigator.'

Prabeena acknowledged the murmurs of assent all around. She had already come to know that Jayanta had been officially assigned this case.

'The show that evening was videographed. They were going to make CDs of the show, and sell them. We've already watched it, right to the end of...the end of her life,' said Jayanta. 'I thought, since you were there, you would know the details. And then the forensics have sent their reports. It's not an accident. Not death by choking, no. It was poison. The details about the poison, and the medical reports, have already reached the others. Prabeena, you will be mailed them, also.'

Prabeena nodded, waiting.

'The paan. Laced liberally with the stuff. Several of them had the poison. Only the top layer, though. The ones underneath only had traces. Spillover.'

'So. This is a murder investigation. Or suicide?' she said, to nobody in particular. She took a breath, and asked, 'Fingerprints?'

'Only hers, on the paandaan. If it was somebody, he or she was careful about that.'

'So many crime thrillers to read and watch, everybody knows about being careful about leaving prints these days,' said a woman officer, sitting near the window.

Sukumar Bose was the first to be questioned. With his hair tied back, he looked much more subdued, less flamboyant than he had onstage the evening of the performance. He answered the questions put to him simply and to the point.

'She was in the small green room by herself most of the time,' he recounted. 'That was her habit. The rest of us were in the larger one. She liked to be alone before a programme, meditating, focussing. We had already rehearsed in the morning at her place, so there was no need to go through everything again.'

'So you wouldn't know if somebody had come in there?' asked Jayanta. 'To meet her?'

'No...not really.'

They all caught the hesitation in his voice.

'Tell us,' said Jayanta.

'Well. The organizers would know better. They did go in once or twice, I saw them through our open door.

And once...' Again the hesitation, but he plunged on, 'The chief guest. He was brought in, I suppose just for a courtesy call, before the programme.'

'Did you know she was pregnant?'

'Who?' The tabla player was confused.

'Shraddha Devi.'

Prabeena felt a twinge of surprise. She glanced at Jayanta, knowing he would be looking at her. He raised his eyebrows imperceptibly, then looked back at Sukumar.

'Pregnant! But she's not married!' he wailed, naively. He took the glass of water that was offered to him and gulped it down, while the others waited.

'No, I didn't know. I mean...Well.' He got a grip on himself, then said, 'I should have guessed. She's been unwell, off and on, these last couple of months. Nothing serious, but several times, rehearsals were cancelled. Nausea, tiredness, that kind of thing.'

'Tell us about her paan habits,' probed Jayanta.

'She choked on the paan, then?' asked Sukumar. Nobody replied. He continued, 'She was quite possessive about the paans. She never shared them with us, you know, even though she was quite generous in other ways. She would get them from some place else, not from here. It wasn't the usual Benarasi or Lucknowi paan. It had a very strong smell. She was addicted to the stuff.'

The other male accompanists said more or less the same things. Iqbal Khan and Rishabh Das had been busy with their own pre-recital routines, but both were sure that very few people had gone into the other green room. Rishabh Das had seen the chief guest being taken in to meet her, but was vague about who else was with him.

'Bring in...' Jayanta glanced down at his iPad, and said, 'Mrinalini. Mrinalini Sharma.'

Close up, the thin taanpura accompanist looked much older than she had onstage. She had a pinched look, but that could have been because of the stress of being called to a police investigation.

'What was your relationship with Shraddha Devi like?' asked Jayanta after the usual questions and answers were done.

She looked startled. 'The normal guru–shishya relationship. Respect, deep respect on my side. Affection on hers.' She looked down at her hands, folded on her lap, as she said this.

Prabeena looked at Jayanta. Getting a nod from him, she asked, 'What did you feel about her rudeness to you onstage?'

Mrinalini glanced quickly at Prabeena, a flash in her eyes, but looked decorously down again. 'Rude. Why rude? No, it is always the Guru's privilege to behave as she likes onstage. She was good to me... we were like a family. We *were* a family. She was younger than me, but I was like her daughter, as far as our musical relationship was concerned,' she added, somewhat ponderously. 'Who would have thought she would choke like that on the paan. She always put them into her mouth throughout the day, and even during recitals. She was habituated to them. Choking on them...unbelievable.'

'You lived with her, I believe?' asked Jayanta.

'Yes. In the true guru–shishya tradition.'

'When was the last time you saw her open the paandaan, the container?' probed Prabeena.

Mrinalini paused. 'Well, we were hardly together after we got to the venue. I don't know...But it was her habit to have a paan on the way to the venue. In the car. She had one while she was going there. She would not touch it during her meditation, but she would have it on stage.' She paused again, and looking up, she asked, 'What does opening the paandaan have to do with her...collapse?'

Nobody answered directly, but the lady police officer near the window asked, 'Do you know anybody who might have a grudge against her? Enough to harm her?'

Mrinalini looked shocked. 'Ah, so...' she left the sentence unfinished. After a pause, she added, 'Well, Guruma had many enemies. There is so much rivalry in this world of shastriya sangeet, you can't imagine. And then she wasn't...' she trailed off.

'She wasn't an easy person to get along with?' finished Prabeena for her.

'I wouldn't exactly go as far as that, maybe, but... well, her domestic staff for instance, they hated her. Mostly, with a couple of exceptions, they keep leaving within a month. She's very autocratic...was...'

'And her pregnancy?' asked Prabeena.

Mrinalini looked sharply at her. 'Well, she had morning sickness, so I guessed.'

'Who do you think…'

'I don't know,' Mrinalini cut her off swiftly. 'She entertained a lot, of course, men also, but they never stayed that long. She did go out often, though. Spending her nights elsewhere. I don't know where, don't ask me. I was not her confidante. Only her student.'

'Please be available for the next few days, we'll let you know if we need something,' said Jayanta.

The committee members were next. The president, Bipul Saikia, a short, tubby man with a worried expression, had met the deceased when she had arrived, and had shown her into her private green room. He had asked if she needed anything. She had said she would let him know if she did. He had then come away, only to return later to escort her to the stage.

'She carried the paandaan to the stage herself?' asked one of the policemen.

'Paandaan?' The man looked puzzled. 'I think so. No, wait. Her two students, the women, they carried her things out from the green room onto the stage. They went in with me to her green room. And then the accompanists, they also came, they also carried some of the stuff. I remember Iqbalji carried the bottle of water. She had a scarf, a white shawl, somebody carried that. I'm not too sure about the paandaan though, I didn't notice.'

'Did anybody else, any outsider, besides the committee members come to meet her while she was in the green room?'

'No, we always guard the privacy of our artistes before a show,' said Saikia, the worry lines increasing on his forehead. 'No members of the public are allowed backstage before a show. After the show, that's a different matter. Autographs and so on.'

'Nobody at all?' probed Jayanta.

'Well, there was the chief guest, of course. But you can hardly...I mean...' The president, a shrewd person, looked from one to the other of them, and asked, 'It's not an accident, then? Choking?'

'The paan was poisoned,' said Jayanta matter-of-factly.

The man said nothing, though the expression in his eyes changed.

'Suicide?'

'I hardly think so. She seemed to be very much in love with life, going by her behaviour onstage. She loved what she was doing, the success that was coming her way.'

'Besides,' said Prabeena, 'I don't think she would have chosen this particular method. To kill herself like that, in full public view...no. She wouldn't want her last moments to be ugly, if she could help it. No, I think suicide...no.'

The full import of what she was saying struck Saikia. 'Murder,' he said quietly.

'So, tell us,' said Jayanta. 'Who else had come

into the green room, then? Yes, this is a murder investigation.'

'Ah. Let me think.' His worry lines deepened. 'That would be Radhika Hazarika, the committee secretary, maybe the assistant secretary also.'

'Nobody else? The tea boy, did she ask for tea, coffee?'

'Ah yes. Probably the catering secretary. Shikha Goswami, along with the tea boy.'

Jayanta consulted his iPad. He nodded.

Radhika Hazarika was calm, precise. Yes, she had come in several times to see if the artiste had needed something. Yes, she had brought in the chief guest at his own request because, he said, she was somebody he knew well. She had brought him to the green room, and left them there alone, because she didn't want to eavesdrop. She had escorted him back to the auditorium when he had emerged.

'How long was he in there?' asked Jayanta.

'Oh about...' She considered. 'Ten minutes.'

Shikha Goswami's story, too, was much the same. She had gone in a couple of times with the tea boy, enquiring if Shraddha Devi wanted something.

'Did she?' asked one of the policemen.

'No. She had her own flask of black tea, it seems. She was sipping from it. She told me it had ginger and black pepper.'

'The tea boy, did he go in alone at any time?'

'No. I took him along with me each time. These artistes, they have such delicate temperaments, one has to be careful...oh, sorry.' She cut herself off, seeming to remember that it was not respectful to speak badly of the dead. But her meaning was clear. Shraddha Devi's manners had probably not been the kind that would endear her immediately to all who came in contact with her.

Prabeena wondered if there would be anybody who would actually mourn Shraddha Devi's death. Not as an artiste, but as a person. While they waited for the next person to be escorted in, Prabeena asked, 'Her family? Who was there in her home?'

'She lived with four of her students in her house in this city. She has family in a village in the interior of deepest Goalpara, but she rarely visited. She didn't encourage them to come here either, it seems. A brother, sister-in-law, a sister, their children. They came for the funeral yesterday, the brother performed the last rites, but they left this morning. Her students, the live-in ones, are the closest she has to family. Not that she seemed to miss having a biological one.'

'Spouse, partner?' probed Prabeena.

'Never married. Many liaisons, though. Nothing permanent. Lots of gossip about her personal life, of which I would say ninety per cent are lies. She enjoyed one-night stands, it seems.'

'No children then?'

'No. This was her first pregnancy.'

'How old was she?'

'Forty-two.'

'Bit late for a pregnancy...but...' She left the rest of her sentence hanging.

'Last person for today,' said Jayanta. 'Jayashree. She uses only one name. A feminist? The other woman on the stage.'

Close up, Jayashree was a beauty. There was something exotic about her looks. She had a hill woman's skin, and faintly slanting eyes. Her hair, now left loose, was straight and black, her mouth a gleaming, rose-tinted pout. She looked at them calmly, taking in their questions one by one.

'Yes, we came in the same car, Guruma, Mrinalinidi and I. No, I don't live in the gurukul with Guruma anymore. I used to, but not for the past few months. I have a flat in the same complex. Yes, I live alone. We went with her to the small green room, kept her things there, and then came back to the large one. She needs...needed...to be alone before a show, for a while.'

'And you carried her stuff from there to the stage, later?' asked Jayanta.

'We all did. There was a lot of stuff. The two taanpuras, digital taanpuras, her bag, shawl...and then of course the harmonium, tablas, sarangi.'

'The paandaan?'

'That, too.'

'Who carried that?'

'Mm. Let me see. I had a taanpura...and...you know, I don't really remember.' She looked back calmly at them, and added, 'It's all such a rush at that time. We touch her feet, get her blessings, get the stuff... sorry, I just don't remember.'

'There are a few more people to interview,' said Jayanta after she left, 'but let's leave that for a bit. Now, to review.' He began to tick off the points on his fingers. 'A. The artiste was not a popular person. So personal hatred could have been a motive. B. The paan that poisoned her was put into the container after she reached the auditorium. Because she had already had a paan in the car. The next one that she had was on the stage. C. Whoever poisoned her knew that she never shared her paans with anybody else. So, somebody close to her did it, knowing that putting the poisoned paan in the container was a precise way of eliminating her. Almost like a well-aimed gun, I would say. Or somebody close to her got it done. D. The victim was alone backstage in the green room for quite some time. Anybody could have got in and done the job, somebody we don't know about. E. She had hardly any close family. Her students say that they were her family, but her treatment of them doesn't seem at all loving.' He looked around the room, and asked, 'Anything else?'

'Motive,' said the policewoman near the window. 'Find the motive, find the murderer.'

'Several, I would think,' said Jayanta, making notes on his iPad. 'Professional hatred. Personal hatred, of which there would be ample amounts, I would imagine. A motive connected to her pregnancy, that's a strong possibility. And maybe other things…which we don't know about, yet…things are still emerging, aren't they?'

Prabeena nodded. 'I was going to ask...did Shraddha Devi leave a will? What properties did she own? Who benefits?'

'Yes, the team is working on that. Her lawyer has been contacted, we'll find out soon. But it won't be her blood family that will benefit, that's my guess.' He looked around the room, then added, 'Okay, let's leave it for now. Things are still coming in. Reports. Interviews.'

People moved around, getting ready to leave. Several came up to Prabeena, greeting her, 'Good to see you, Prabs, it's been a while!' They took care, all of them, not to look at Jayanta as they asked, 'How's Himangshu, then? Busy at the univ? I hear he's recently published another book of poetry. Must read it!'

Prabeena knew they never would. They would not even, in their stressed and busy lives, get around to buying it. But she was grateful to them for making her feel welcome and including Himangshu in the welcome, too.

With a small change in his facial expression, Jayanta signalled to her to wait. 'I'm off to interview the chief guest, Ranjit Choudhury. I didn't want it to be a crowd. Would you...ah...' Suddenly diffident, he added formally, 'If you are interested, perhaps you might care to accompany me there? Your professional appraisal will be valuable...'

On the way to Ranjit Choudhury's office in Jayanta's car, Prabeena came to know several things about the evening's chief guest, based on the background checks that his team had done. A wealthy businessman, but she had guessed that already. After all, chief guests at these cultural shows, she had learnt in these months with Himangshu, were usually moneybags who could be expected to contribute to the expenses. In return, they got the ego massage of being welcomed on stage, and being made much of. Certainly, not all chief guests, nor all businessmen or moneyed people were like that. But Ranjit Choudhury, industrialist, was one such.

'We've also done background checks on the other people we met today,' continued Jayanta. The driver and security man sitting in the front seat were trusted people, and he knew that what he spoke would remain confidential. 'Some interesting stuff. Sukumar Bose loves to bet on horses. He's been losing a lot lately. Iqbal Khan has an expensive hobby, collecting old musical instruments. Where does he get that kind of money? Well, okay, their professional lives are busy, money is flowing in, but still, that line might be worth investigating. Mrinalini, ummm...how to put this, she's a porn addict. Late night viewings on laptops in the gurukul, I believe. And the beauteous Jayashree lives in magnificent opulence in a flat that's all paid for. Her income from her music is surely not enough to fund this? The committee secretary, she's sending her daughter to a pricey school. Does she have her hand in the till? Ah, human nature! But is any of this motive enough to actually murder the lady?'

'Everybody needs money. But that doesn't make them murderers,' agreed Prabeena.

They kept their conversation professional. It was easier that way.

They were ushered into Ranjit Choudhury's office with some ceremony. He received them cordially, even effusively. After the fuss about teas and coffees was over, and they were seated, he said, leaning towards them across the desk, 'Terrible thing, about Shraddha. Terrible. Who would have thought...and the media! They're just going berserk. As though it's some kind of tamasha. An entertainment.'

'How well did you know her?' asked Jayanta.

'Personally? Not all that well. Of course I am... was...an admirer of her music. Who wouldn't be?'

'Did you meet her last evening? Alone?'

'Yes, I believe we were alone for a little bit, in the green room. I went to wish her...'

'She was flirting with you, wasn't she?' asked Prabeena. 'Onstage.'

He looked at her, expressionless.

'Yes, I was there. Sitting just behind you.'

'Ah. Well, that's part of the tradition, isn't it? To be coquettish, flirtatious...'

'Really? I've heard several thumri and dadra singers. Girija Devi, Shobha Gurtu, Rita Ganguli... nobody flirted like this.' She hadn't, actually, but had heard Himangshu talking about them. About their music, their dedication to their art.

There was silence. Jayanta broke it, asking, 'So did you talk about her pregnancy while you were there?'

The man's demeanour changed completely. His

face seemed to collapse, his shoulders sagged. They watched him, silently, as he reached out for a glass of water. Finally, he said, 'Yes. Briefly.'

'Did you know about it before that?'

Ranjit Choudhury hesitated, then said, 'Look. I'll be honest. Yes, we used to meet. Quite regularly. But I wasn't the only one she met, I know that. Anyway. She called me the morning of the concert, and told me that she was pregnant.'

'And...'

'And that I was responsible. She said she would meet me in the evening, before the show.'

'Did you have...words with her?'

'You mean, did we have an argument? No. I told her in the green room that we would talk later. Today, in fact. And then that accident.'

'It wasn't an accident,' said Jayanta. 'She was poisoned.'

Ranjit Choudhury was silent. Finally, he said, 'I see. The water?'

'The paan,' said Jayanta. 'Actually, I wanted to ask you. You would know. Where did she get them? They were not the usual meetha paan. She needed a steady supply. Who got them for her?'

'I really wouldn't know,' said Ranjit Choudhury.

'You're lying,' thought Prabeena. But neither of them said anything further as they took their leave.

In the car again, Prabeena asked, 'What about his family? Wife, somebody who would be very angry if she came to know her husband was the father of Shraddha Devi's child?'

'Choudhury would not want this to be made public not so much because of the wife, but because he has political ambitions. Something like this would be blown up no end when elections come around. He's hoping to get a ticket.'

Jayanta looked at his iPad, and added, 'Okay, some more reports. I had asked for information on Shraddha Devi's movements over the last month.'

'And...?'

He looked up at her. 'The usual. Shops. Banks. Spas. Doctor, but that's understandable in the light of what we now know. Lawyer. Concerts, her own and other peoples', radio and other recordings. Travel. But...' he paused, 'Tell me, isn't this guru–shishya tradition supposed to be hierarchical? I mean, would a teacher go every evening, almost, to her student's house? Every evening that she was in town? That too, late at night? Returning in the early hours?'

Prabeena waited. But instead of continuing, he told the driver, 'We won't be going back to the office, Sujit. Take us to this address.' He consulted his iPad again, and gave him an address.

~

Jayashree looked surprised to see them when she opened the door to her penthouse. It was a huge, spacious place, airy, bright with light and fresh houseplants. It was done up in steel and glass. The furnishings were either black or white. At one end of the vast living room was a large bar.

'Sorry to barge in like this,' said Jayanta formally. He looked around. 'You're alone?'

'Yes, I live alone, I told you.'

'No maids, nothing?'

'No live-in help. People come in for cooking and cleaning, off and on through the day. They have their own keys.'

Jayashree must have returned immediately, and changed. In her tiny shorts and cropped top, she didn't look at all like a student of shastriya sangeet now. She didn't ask them to sit down, but they did, anyway, and made themselves comfortable on a zebra-striped couch.

After the preliminary questions, Prabeena leaned forward and asked, 'You live here alone?'

'Yes, I've told you several times.'

'Just stick to the point please, no extra comments,' said Prabeena, her voice hard. 'You rent it? Or is it yours?'

The girl looked at them. 'It's mine,' she said finally.

'It must have cost quite a bit, a huge place like this. And poshly furnished!'

Jayashree said nothing. Prabeena stared at her for a moment, then got up and went towards a passage that led off from the bar. Doors opened on either side of it. She opened a door on the left.

The room was covered in mirrors. The ceiling, the walls, everything. A circular bed, with an ornate throw was positioned in the centre. The furniture, the upholstery, everything was pink. It was obvious what this room was being used for.

She went to the other rooms. Three bedrooms, one each on either side of the corridor. At one end of the penthouse was the largest one. It was all done in marble and glass, though the colour scheme here was black and gold. Huge TV screens, with stacks of DVDs under them. Prabeena took out one. The picture on it was of two girls and a man, all unclothed, in explicit poses. Porn. She took up a few more from the stacks at random. They all had the same kind of pictures, the only variations being in the poses.

She opened one of the cupboards. One shelf was stacked with plastic containers of various shapes and sizes, placed neatly. She took out one, and looked at the unfamiliar object. She turned it around in her hand. It was battery operated. She put on the little switch at the side. The object began to throb in her hand. She realized what it was. A vibrator.

She took out one or two other containers. They were all, she realized, sex toys. There was a variety of them, some of which she could not fathom the use of. She put them back on the shelf, glancing back once to look at Jayashree, who had followed her into the room. The girl's face remained expressionless.

There was also a video camera. Even without examining it, Prabeena knew that it was quite state-of-the-art. Expensive, without a doubt. She examined the door of the cupboard closely. Yes, there it was. An aperture, placed just at the level of a shelf which was at the same height, more or less, as the bed.

She returned to the living room. Jayanta was at the

bar, looking closely at the shelves that lined the wall behind it. Prabeena saw that it was very well stocked. But Jayanta was not examining the bottles. He was, instead, touching the shelves. He had taken out a few bottles, and was looking at the wall that lay exposed.

He nodded to Prabeena as she came out. 'Have to get back to the office, Prabs, some reports have come in.' He looked at Jayashree, and said formally, 'Please be available for the next few days. We may be calling you, and others too, for questioning again.'

'I have an out of town concert next week,' she said.

'Next week. Okay, we'll see. Get in touch with us in any case.'

~

In the car, Prabeena said, 'It's furnished like a cat house. You should see the bedrooms...high-end. All kinds of gadgets. And a video camera to film the action. Through a peephole. In secret, I think, without the people knowing? Perhaps.'

'It figures,' said Jayanta. 'The living room is bugged. Quite sophisticated, the gadgetry.'

'Blackmail?' wondered Prabeena. 'Jayashree, running a pretty little racket? Lure in the people with her stunning looks. I suppose she has other girls who work this thing. And then blackmail the clients, after showing them the videos, into parting with vast sums of money? It's an angle that bears investigation.'

'I'll get someone to question the security people at the entrance,' said Jayanta. 'Meanwhile, there's been a call from Ranjit Choudhury. He wanted to speak to me, personally, about something, he said. He sounded nervous.'

Back at his office, Ranjit Choudhury was waiting for them. The fuss over the tea and coffee was minimal this time.

'Okay,' he said. He paused, and Prabeena saw that he had taken a deep breath before he continued. 'Here's the thing. The media have somehow got wind of the fact of Shraddha's death being a murder. They have come to know about my links to her. They were here a while ago, asking me all kinds of questions.'

Jayanta and Prabeena waited. To fill the silence, the policeman murmured, 'Ah, the media. A dramatic case like this, of course they'll be interested.'

'I...okay. Here's what I wanted to tell you. In confidence.' Ranjit Choudhury seemed to have decided what to say. 'If I may be frank...'

They waited.

'See, they don't know anything about Shraddha's pregnancy yet. Or that, you know, I might be the probable father. I just want to request you, could you please keep that under wraps? The Assembly elections are due in a few months, and the nominations for the party I've been working with are due any day. I've been promised the nomination for this city, but with this scandal breaking around me, obviously my party won't risk it.'

'It is a murder, after all,' said Prabeena, unable to keep quiet. 'Naturally they will not give you a nomination.'

'Naturally,' said Ranjit Choudhury, though he looked unhappy. The words came out half-heartedly. 'Anyway, my request to you, please consider it. And also,' he looked directly at Prabeena, 'there's my wife. She's an invalid. This shock might be too much for her, too much.'

If he was looking for sympathy from Prabeena, he didn't succeed.

'The media, they are very persistent,' said Jayanta in a calm voice. 'Of course, no leaks will come from my office, I can assure you of that. But then there are so many other links, so many people in the know. Who knows what they might say?'

'For instance,' added Prabeena smoothly, 'when you went to meet her at that love nest. Were there any other people around who might know?'

'Ummm. Jayashree, the girl who lives there. It's her place, I believe.'

'You do know, of course, that your trysts were videographed?'

The man looked at her, astonished. He opened his mouth, but seemed unable to speak. He reached out a trembling hand and took the glass of water beside him, gulping it down quickly. Finally, he said, 'No, I didn't know. Who? Not Shraddha, I'm pretty sure of that.'

'How can you be so sure?' asked Prabeena.

'Because she, Shraddha, was not a scheming kind of person. I've known her for a while. She was an artiste, don't forget, a renowned one. She didn't really need the money she would have got from blackmail.

Besides, she was in it for the fun of it. She enjoyed...'
he broke off, had some more water, and said, 'Maybe
that girl, Jayashree...'

'Has she approached you in any way?' asked
Prabeena.

'Blackmail, you mean?' The man's voice was
stronger now. 'No. Not yet. But it's a weapon she has
in her hands. Maybe,' he turned to them hopefully,
'you could seize them, the videos?'

'Not much point in that,' said Jayanta. 'In my
experience, the first thing blackmailers do is make
multiple copies of the material they intend to use.'
He stood up and stretched out his hand to Ranjit
Choudhury. 'Okay, we have to move. If there's
anything you need to speak about, we are at your
service.'

'That's one nervous man now,' observed Prabeena
in the car. 'Do you think he's telling the truth, though?'

'About the video? And the blackmail?' Jayanta
was silent for a moment. Thoughtfully, he added, 'He
will, of course, know the implications. As a blackmail
victim, he would be the first suspect in a murder, no
matter how strongly he insists that he didn't know
about it. Or that Shraddha Devi was in the dark
about it, too.'

'True,' said Prabeena. 'And in any case, all
politicians, even aspiring politicians, are very good
actors, aren't they?'

'Okay, I'm calling it a day now, I need to think,'
said Jayanta. 'Come home?' he added hopefully. 'We
can have dinner together, and I'll drop you home.'

'Actually, why don't we go to my house?' said Prabeena. 'I'm offering you dinner. It's evening already. Yes, Bina will have cooked something nice, I'm sure, and you look as though you need a drink.'

Himangshu opened the door to their home when Prabeena rang the bell. 'Jayanta, how nice to see you, do come in, please.'

They went out to the back terrace which overlooked the university campus nearby. It was dark all around, but it was lit by solar-powered lamps, which created pools of light amid the dark shadows of the trees. The breeze was soothing as they clinked their glasses. Bina hovered near them, passing around freshly grilled kebabs.

It didn't take them very long to get back to the ease of previous times, before the divorce, when they had all sat companionably together on many evenings. Himangshu had been a friend of both Jayanta and Prabeena, and all three had enjoyed each other's company—before friendship turned into love for Prabeena and Himangshu. Jayanta popped a kebab into his mouth, and said, mock sadly to the cook, 'You know, Bina, I have somehow managed to get over the fact that your baideo,' he nodded in Prabeena's direction, 'decided to leave. But you, no. I shall always miss you, Bina. You can still come back, you know, your room at the back is still empty.'

'Who cooks for you, then, saar?' asked Bina, pausing as she handed out plates of freshly steamed pork momos. She was genuinely concerned.

'Well, a lady comes in, and then there are the police orderlies who come and go. But there's nothing like your cooking...' Drink had made him quite maudlin.

Prabeena had filled in Himangshu on the events of the day. 'Complicated,' he commented when she had finished. 'And she was pregnant, you say? Imagine!'

'Yes.'

'Hmm. Then it would be quite easy to find the murderer, surely?' he asked.

Prabeena was intrigued. 'How do you mean, Himu?'

'Well, all you...we have to do is find out whose fortunes would change once the baby was born. Whose lifestyle, whose prestige would be threatened.'

'That would be Ranjit, of course. The father. Or the purported father. But he denies murdering her. Of course. But somehow I'm inclined to believe him. I hardly see him going into the green room and putting in poisoned paans while Shraddha Devi watched him. No, I don't think he got the opportunity, actually.'

'So, okay, it's somebody else. Somebody who we don't know much about yet, maybe?'

'I'm laying out the food, baideo,' called Bina from the dining room. 'When I saw Jayanta saar had come, I made khaar, and also fish tenga, just as he used to like it.'

They went into the dining room, and talked of other things. Food, cuisine, music, all the many things that old friends did when they met up after a long time.

~

Jayanta and Prabeena met again at his office next day. They reviewed the recorded statements of all those who had been questioned, going over them minutely.

'You know, Prabs,' said Jayanta, finally. He leaned back in his chair, and continued, 'I'm beginning to think Himangshu was right.'

Prabeena looked questioningly at him.

'Find the person whose life would change because of the coming baby. And then you have the culprit. The motive.'

'Let's go visit her home, I think? There may be something there.'

Shraddha Devi's large apartment was in the same complex where Jayashree had her pad. 'The boys have been here, they've asked around, it's all there in the report that was mailed to you,' Jayanta had said on the way there.

'Even so. A first-hand recce might throw up something.'

A woman, obviously the domestic help, let them in. While Jayanta showed her his police credentials, Prabeena looked around. Yes, this certainly looked like an artiste's home. There were pictures of Shraddha Devi performing in venues around the world, being felicitated by dignitaries at prestigious functions. There were plaques and other memorabilia commending her performances.

Beyond the living and dining area, two rooms had been combined to make a large space. The music room. It was full of instruments. Shrouded shapes that

Prabeena realized were taanpuras leaned against the wall. There were two harmoniums and several pairs of tablas on the durrie-covered floor.

Of the other rooms, one was obviously Shraddha Devi's bedroom. It was quite spartan, with minimal furniture. The only things that spoke of lavishness was a state-of-the-art music system, and a large LED TV. One wall was lined with cupboards, but Prabeena did not open them. On the bedside table were a copy of the Gita, and a photograph of an elderly man with a surmandal. Probably her Guru, surmised Prabeena. Beside these was a small silver box.

The maid noticed Prabeena looking curiously at the receptacle. 'It's her paan box, ma'am,' she said. 'Not the main one that she always carried around with her. That's with the police, I believe,' she added, looking at Jayanta. 'This is the one she kept here. Sometimes she would have a paan before going to sleep.'

Prabeena took the box and opened it. It was like a book, with the covers on both sides opening out to reveal little compartments inside. One side contained cloves, cinnamon and other stuff in the compartments. The other cover opened to reveal several paan leaves, as well as raw betel nut. It had a strong, pungent smell that Prabeena found distasteful. How could anyone be addicted to this stuff? she thought, replacing the box, with its contents intact, where she had found it.

The maid noticed her distaste. 'It's very strong, ma'am, but she was addicted to it. She needed to get a fresh supply very frequently, it spoils very fast. I should be cleaning that box out, but I don't feel like disturbing anything in this room, not yet...'

'Where did she get them from?'asked Prabeena.

'I'm not sure,' said the maid. 'People come and go all the time here. I'm in the kitchen most of the time. I really wouldn't know.'

'And she, your baideo, she would come and go at all hours, would she?'

The maid looked indignant at what she felt was an unfair imputation. 'She was a very famous singer. Of course she came and went at all hours. Her concerts took place at night, after all. And then sometimes she would go to other places. Other peoples' baithaks, other peoples' concerts, to listen. In any case, my duty ends at ten here. I go to my room on the roof, and sleep.'

Prabeena got the impression that she had been firmly put in her place by this maid, loyal to her difficult mistress even after her death. She smiled in a placatory manner, and moved out of the room.

The other, smaller bedrooms housed the students. A single room for Mrinalini, with a bed, a table, and a taanpura. The other bedroom had two beds, for the other two students, supposed Prabeena.

She turned to the maid who was following them around anxiously, and asked, 'Where are they? The students? Mrinalini?'

'They've gone across the road to get some groceries, they said. Shall I call them? I have their numbers.'

'No need,' said Prabeena, in a preoccupied tone. There was something that she couldn't quite put her finger to, something that had been triggered by something here.

Once outside the building, she turned to Jayanta and said, 'Since we are here, let's go across to the beauteous Jayashree's pad again. Let's see...'

Once more, Jayashree looked surprised to see them. She was dressed in skinny jeans this time, with a white shirt. She looked fresh and pretty. Without asking her permission, they went in, and sat down once more on the zebra-striped couch in the living room. Jayashree followed them in, and stood before them, her eyes watchful.

Prabeena looked around and said to the girl, 'So. Quite a pretty set-up here. You're the madame? Or just the caretaker?'

'It's not like that,' said the girl. She still hadn't lost her cockiness. 'It's not what you think.'

'Ah, so,' said Prabeena, settling into the couch, 'Tell us. What should we think?' She turned to Jayanta, who had just finished taking a call.

'No, nothing like that. It's just...Guruma liked to come here, to relax. She would spend evenings here.'

'With different men? Ranjit Choudhury, and who else?'

It was now that the girl began to look uneasy. 'They appreciated her music,' she said defensively.

Prabeena realised what had been bothering her ever since she had seen the music room in Shraddha Devi's apartment. One of the things, of several.

'Ah! Appreciated her music. How is it then that I haven't seen a single musical instrument here? No taanpura, no harmonium ? If the baithaks were in this large room, there should be several taanpuras, tablas, the lot?

'They are there. In my room,' she nodded towards the other end of the house. 'I do my riyaz there, she used them when she came here.' She got up and opened the door to a room at the far end. In the corner, beyond the bed, Prabeena saw the harmonium and taanpura.

'Only one, though. Her own home has several, each student has one in his or her room. A famous artiste, a place used for baithaks, and only one taanpura? It doesn't match.'

Jayanta's cell rang again. He went near the bar, and spoke in low tones.

'Okay, Jayashree, tell me about yourself,' continued Prabeena. 'You are from which place?'

'Shillong,' she said.

'And how long have you been here?'

'Five, almost six years now.'

'Shillong, hmmm,' said Prabeena. Something, some memory niggled her mind again, but she couldn't quite place it. 'And do you go there often?'

'Off and on, yes.'

'How often? Once a month? Once a week?'

'Once a week, about that,' she said grudgingly. 'Leaving your riyaz, everything aside. I see. Isn't that too often for a shastriya sangeet student who needs to practise for hours every day? Too many breaks, I would think. You have family there?'

'Yes. Family. Friends.'

Jayanta came back, the cell phone still in his hand. He switched it off, and put it inside his pocket.

'This flat, it's in your name, all right. But of course you didn't pay for it, did you?' he asked, his eyes narrowing as he gazed at her.

Jayashree stared at him, not saying anything.

'It was paid for by Shraddha Devi. A large sum of money, of course, but then she could afford it, a highly regarded artiste like her. Then she gifted it to you, through a deed. Why? I think the answer's obvious—she used you as a front.'

Jayashree looked down at her hands. Prabeena noticed the shell pink nail polish. In a low voice, Jayashree said, 'She wanted a kotha, she said. Something like what it was in the old days, the days of the tawaifs. The nautch girls. That's how it was meant to be. She said it would make her look bad if it was in her name, and people found out. The deal was that I would take care of it, and she would pay me a stipend.'

They waited, without saying anything.

'But it really never was. It was just her and her friends. Men friends. Sometimes one, sometimes more.'

'Ah. And you, what would you be doing?' asked Prabeena.

'Serving them drinks, snacks, dinner, that kind of thing. We couldn't keep full-time help. They would gossip. It was just me in the evenings. After they went to one of the bedrooms, I would go to mine.

They would let themselves out later. Sometimes the man would stay till the morning. I would give him breakfast, and he would leave.'

'And she would come here, and entertain her guest, even while she was pregnant?'

Jayashree looked quickly at her, then looked away again. 'No.'

'So she's not been here for the past few weeks, at least, is that it?' asked Prabeena. She added, 'It will be easier if you tell us the truth. We are cross-checking everything, you know, and the security man downstairs has a very good memory of all comings and goings.'

The girl said slowly, 'She came once, no twice I think. In the daytime. I took my music lessons from her then.'

'And the videos? Did Shraddha Devi know that you were quietly filming her, and the men? Was she in on it?'

The girl did not hesitate. 'I really don't know what you are talking about,' she said evenly.

'But of course you do,' said Prabeena pleasantly, 'We'll get to the bottom of it. We always do.'

'This concert next week, just cancel it, please,' said Jayanta. 'And be available. At all times. Keep your cell switched on.'

'It will be very difficult...' began Jayashree. But she stopped when she saw the look on the police officer's face.

Back in the car, Jayanta said, 'Whose life would change if—when—the baby came into the picture?'

He ticked off the names. 'Ranjit Choudhury. It would be a time bomb, ticking away, growing up maybe to resemble him and ruining his chances of becoming a big shot in politics.'

He looked at Prabeena, and continued, 'The students, to some extent. Probably the present gurukul set-up would not continue, not in this form, if there was a little baby around. But I doubt that the students would kill for that.'

'Unlikely,' agreed Prabeena. She looked at Jayanta with amusement, and said, 'Okay, just say it, why are you pussyfooting around the name.'

He laughed. 'Yes, well, of course, Jayashree. Her life would change. Shraddha Devi's visits would not continue, at least for a while. But,' he frowned, 'how would that change her life? After all, the flat is hers, legally.'

They looked at each other, considering. 'The blackmail—since that was the ultimate plan, I guess,' Prabeena said thoughtfully.

'But she didn't really need Shraddha for that. She could have brought in her own customers, got herself a ring of high-end call girls who would operate from there,' pointed out Jayanta.

'One minute, Jayanta,' broke in Prabeena, her voice edged with some certainty. 'Remember you gave an update on Shraddha Devi's movements in the last few days before her death?'

'Yes, I have the report, here we are—' he looked through the iPad and recounted. 'Shops, friends, concerts, the usual. Her doctor...and lawyer.' He looked up, and said, 'The boys have done preliminary questioning of all of them already. But...'

'Yes. More on the lawyer.'

'I'll send the boy who did the investigation.'

'No, let's go there ourselves, Jayanta,' said Prabeena.

~

A few hours later, they were back in Jayashree's house. It was a long time before she opened the door, this time. She didn't seem surprised to see them anymore.

It felt quite natural to go straight to the zebra-striped couch and make themselves comfortable there. The lady of the house stood silently before them, beauteous as always, but, Prabeena noticed, something had changed in her demeanour. Nothing obvious, she still looked confident, but there was, this time, an undercurrent of wariness in her stance.

Without preamble, Jayanta asked, his voice quite normal, 'You knew, of course, that she was preparing to change her will? This house, all the property and money that she owned, would have gone to the unborn child. She was going to make arrangements to get it back, this house. You would no longer be the owner of this place. Not even on paper. And she would no longer give you the money that she used to.'

'I don't know what you're talking about,' replied Jayashree in a low voice.

'We've just come back from the office of the lawyer

who was arranging it,' said Jayanta. 'Yes, this house is in your name, but nothing is irrevocable, not even a gift deed. She was planning to get the house back, and put it, ultimately, in the name of the child after it was born. The paperwork would have been completed next week. You must have overheard her on the phone, or maybe she told you about her plans herself. She was quite euphoric about the baby, I believe.'

'I really don't know anything of all that. You can't prove anything and anyway, I was going to call you. I need to go to Shillong. I have an important function there, and then a dinner has been arranged.'

Something clicked in Prabeena's brain, the missing bit that she had been searching for.

'All right.' She addressed Jayashree, but she was looking at Jayanta as she spoke. 'The men. You said you gave them dinner when they came here. Complete with paan? You can't have a kotha, even a rudimentary kotha, without paan, right? Of course!'

The girl was looking at her now, her eyes wide with something very like fear.

'And your frequent trips to Shillong. *That's* why you would go,' continued Prabeena. 'To get fresh stocks of that hill paan and tamol. Probably, like all paan lovers, she needed fresh stocks of that variety, and that is only available in Meghalaya. Kwai, I believe it's called. It's difficult to get it here, what you do get is a little wilted. It's very strong. Pungent. And addictive. Shraddha Devi was addicted to that, wasn't she? And she had to have it every day, even,' she drew closer to Jayashree, 'even when she was performing onstage.'

The girl stood up, looking this way and that, terror in her eyes.

'You were, actually, in charge of the paandaan. It was part of your duties to keep it filled. And carry it around.'

'Really, I...'

But Prabeena continued, relentlessly, 'And that's another thing. You handled the container, you carried it in, but your fingerprints were not there. Wiped clean. But they should have been there, legitimately, hmm?'

Jayashree was staring at her now, her eyes glazing with fear.

'And it's so easy to get poison these days,' Prabeena continued. 'You knew her habits well, who better. You placed the poisoned paans in her paandaan after she had had one in the car. Maybe in the green room, maybe while going onto the stage. You were carrying it, anyway. You wanted her death to be a public one, you wanted it to be in full view of her lover.'

With a small animal sound, Jayashree started to run towards the door. But Jayanta was ready. He cut her off efficiently, and held her squirming body till resistance stopped.

He set her down on the sofa. 'Watch her, Prabs, will you? The team is waiting just outside the door. I'll call them to take her away.'

~

Two evenings later.

All three were sitting once more in Prabeena's and Himangshu's terrace with their drinks, while Bina plied them with freshly fried besan-coated brinjal fritters and fried fish fingerlings.

'How tasty this is, Bina,' said Jayanta appreciatively. 'My orderly, Abdul, he tries, but poor guy...'

Bina glowed, and looked at Prabeena, who smiled back.

They talked about all the other things in their lives, the beauty of music, of literature and art, the pleasures of dining on fish fresh from the ghat. Finally, they came around to the topic of the case.

'There's one thing I don't understand, though,' said Himangshu, taking their glasses to fill them up again. 'I had thought that once you gifted a person something, that is, legally gifted something, you couldn't revoke it. You couldn't take it back. So how...'

'Ah, that's the thing,' said Jayanta, leaning back on the cushions of his cane chair. 'It's really...' he took another fried brinjal, 'Shraddha Devi, in spite of being such a gifted artiste, was also a canny soul. Not the stereotype of the other-worldy artiste at all. You see, Shraddha Devi's gift was not a Gift Simpliciter which cannot be unilaterally revoked. Shraddha Devi's gift actually was what is known as a Conditional Gift Deed stipulating that the gift would be conditional to Jayashree rendering maintenance and future services to Shraddha Devi. Upon Shraddha's death, the gift would be absolute. Under the law such an arrangement, that is, the Conditional Gift Deed would be revokable by the donor on the grounds that the services that the beneficiary had agreed to provide, were not being provided. Shraddha Devi hadn't burnt her bridges when she had had her lawyer draw up the gift deed. However, if the donor were to die before it was revoked, and before the donor had signed the Deed of Cancellation, the earlier beneficiary stood to get the gift. And Jayashree knew the terms of the gift, that it was revocable, knew also that after her discussion with her lawyer, her Guru was making arrangements to revoke the deed. So she took matters into her own hands before that could take place.'

For a while, the three of them were silent. Only the breeze plying through the trees in the park sighed around them, sounding like the low-pitched drone of a softly played taanpura.

GINNY KALRA, I LOVED YOU

Pratyaksha

Bali is purring loudly. She looks at me with huge green eyes. She is not my cat. Rather, she is the fifth floor cat. There are three of us on the fifth floor. Ginny Kalra across and the Mudgaonkars on the other side. The flat next to mine is mostly locked up. Someone comes and goes for sure but in my one year here I have never seen that person. Sometimes I can hear the shower running and sometimes a muffled voice. The wall between our flats is only five inches thick. I can tap tap and hear an answering tap tap. Sometimes I wish Ginny Kalra lived in that apartment. Then we could talk in Morse code in the night.

Ginny Kalra is an air hostess. She has been here much longer than me. She flies to New York and Stockholm and Rio and Vegas. When she is in town, we spend a lot of time together. She is very tall, fair and slim as a reed with blonde streaks in her short cropped hair.

We sit and drink wine from small bottles bought from duty free shops and laugh a lot. She gets funny stuff for me. Perfumes and toiletries that she picks up from hotel rooms. Sometimes chocolates and fridge magnet stickers proclaiming 'I love Rio' or 'I love Vegas' or 'Paris Je t'aime'.

The Mudgaonkars keep to themselves. They are in their sixties. She is corpulent, always dressed in an oversized maxi dress with a stole draped around her heavy bosom and he, fit as a fiddle and still quite handsome in knee-length shorts and tight T-shirts. I have often seen her peeping from behind the curtain of the window that looks out onto the landing, but the moment I look towards her, the curtain is hurriedly drawn as if no one was ever there. I can sense her, though, from behind the curtain, her heavy frame silhouetted against the thin fabric.

Just below my flat lives Percy. Percy the tall, Percy the drooping, Percy the silent disapproval. If I hang out from my bedroom window I can see a bit of his balcony. That day my skirt fell down from the railing of my balcony and got stuck in the wire stretched across his, I rang the bell and Mrs Delnaz opened the door. I stuttered, 'My skirt...'

'Come in, come in...' Mrs Delnaz opened the door wide and I could see into the flat. The hall was chock-a-block with heavy carved furniture. Sofas and deep chairs and dresser drawers. Mrs Delnaz's daughter Shireen sat in her wheelchair, smiling vacantly.

'My skirt...?' I stuttered again as Mrs Delnaz pushed me into a chair. 'Tea? Biscuits...? Jamset... Jamset...?' Mrs Delnaz rambles on. Jamset is the teenage nephew. I know him because he's always lurking in the stairway.

I can see my skirt fluttering on the wire across the hall. Resolutely I declare, no, Mrs Delnaz, thank you, but no tea, just my skirt, and march towards the balcony, grab my skirt and march out.

I can sense MrsDelnaz wringing her hands and smiling a dilute smile and muttering apologetically, 'Maybe you can come later for tea...'

~

I like Shireen. She is pretty and sweet. But she has some problem with her legs. She can't walk. As a result, she is mostly depressed. When she is cheerful, it can be good fun to talk to her. But otherwise it is best to steer clear. Mrs Delnaz is another matter though. She must have been quite a beauty when she was younger but now she looks like a faded comical version, a caricature. Her hair has thinned into tiny wisps and her face has lost all its contours. It is only from the black and white pictures adorning the living room wall that one can make out how pretty and elegant she once was.

I come back to my room and spend the Sunday doing nothing. Ginny is out. She may come back next week. I sit and moon about Percy. I have a hunch Ginny too is soft on him even though she has all the handsome pilots and stewards to flirt with. But Percy is something else. He works in some foreign bank. He is mostly very aloof, very handsome, very full of attitude and full of contempt for us, the two giggly young girls

When Ginny comes back four days later, we are up the whole night. Her body clock is all awry and since I have been bored the whole week, I don't mind staying up. She is wearing very short shorts. She stretches out her long bronzed legs and crosses them in front of her. They seem endless to me. Ginny is svelte and stunning. I am podgy and plain. And to forget that I eat more chocolates and drink more wine that she has brought. We talk about sex, the different postures. I have never had sex but my imagination is quite fertile. I make up in that department what my lack of experience doesn't. It's almost three in the morning when I stagger back to my flat. I am humming, 'Falling', the Peter Blake song, and feeling fudgy happy at the seams. It takes me hours to fit my key in the door and open it.

～

My head is splitting open and someone is hammering relentlessly at my temples.

I mumble, stop, stop. My eyelids are glued shut and I use my fingers to pry them open.

'What the fuck…?'

The door bell is ringing. I stagger out and there is a crowd outside. Someone pulls at me and I walk, zombie-like, into Ginny Kalra's flat. Into her tiny bathroom. Into the bathtub. Into the blood that is everywhere.

I scream and black out.

～

Inspector Ruby Ghorpade is very business-like, very stern. But despite her sternness she looks like the next-door amma. Comfortably fat and rounded, a nose pin on her blob of a nose, and brown twinkling eyes.

'So, tell me miss…your name first?'

'Elena D'souza,' I mumble. My mouth is full of ash. My eyes hurt; my stomach is a mass of knots.

'So, Miss Elena D'souza, tell us when was the last time you saw the victim?'

'What victim?'

'Ginny Kalra.' She is not the amma next door. Anymore.

'Last night.' My voice is a whisper.

'Why did you do it?'

I concentrate on her bulges. Her uniform is straining at her tummy. The buttons look ready to pop. I am fascinated by the buttons. In my numb state I begin to recall the crime films that I have seen.

'I want to call my lawyer.' (What lawyer? I do not know any lawyer.)

They tell me later that I fainted, blacked out. An excess of chocolate, alcohol and murder can make anyone go round the bend. Potent cocktail, yes sir.

'Shock and trauma,' the doctor says in a dry monotone.

Percy is with me in the hospital.

He takes me back to his house. Mrs Delnaz fusses around me. Jamset is nowhere to be seen.

Inspector Ghorpade has warned everyone that she will come again, soon.

Ginny's flat is cordoned off. The door is sealed. I hanker after the rust silk scarf that she had bought for me, and the perfume, the purple Davidoff. I had left them on the couch when I had left in a drunken stupor in the wee hours. I am concentrating on the perfume bottle. Both of us had dabbed it on our wrists. The fragrance still lingers.

They say Constable Naik had noticed the smell. The smell of the five-star hotel madamji, he had exclaimed, the young lad from the seventh floor reported.

I sleep in Shireen's room.

Her body lay in the bathtub. Her throat slit. The blood all over. She lay as if she was sleeping. Her limbs arranged properly, her ankles crossed and her hands folded on her stomach that was stained red.

Obviously someone had done this to her. That is, slit her throat, stabbed her and arranged her limbs.

The investigation team are leafing through the semi-porn magazines in her bedroom. Laughing. Cussing salaciously, a vicarious voyeurism coursing through their veins

Inspector Ruby Ghorpade asks, 'Who was her lover? Who was she sleeping around with? Tell me, Elena, you will be saved a lot of trouble.'

They have found my fingerprints all over. On the glass, on the bottle, on the magazine and the door knobs, in her bathroom, even. I remember the last pee there. I had flushed the cistern. I had washed my hands, then picked up the hand lotion, I had touched the mirror.

'I know nothing, nothing,' I tremble and cry. Percy is with me all the time. Jamset tells me Mrs Mudgaonkar was telling the downstairs neighbour that she had seen me coming out furtively from Ginny's flat in the morning.

When I go up to my flat I meet her on the landing. She gives me a hostile look.

The news has been on the television channels ever since. Ginny Kalra, the beautiful air hostess, murdered brutally in her Matunga flat. They flash her pictures. Smiling into the camera with two other air hostesses. Some file picture. Another of her, a pouting selfie, and another holidaying in Ibiza. The last two taken from her Facebook.

They talk about her last status update, 'Life is so beautiful I could die.'

The anchor whispers dramatically, she almost had a premonition of death. A life cut short, a brilliant career snuffed out.

Then someone discovers she had changed her relationship status from 'single' to 'in a relationship'.

Tell us about the boyfriend then,' Inspector Ruby Ghorpade coaxes me. 'Come on, tell us all you know.'

'This is news to me. She never told me about any boyfriend,' I mumble

'Really, then what you talked the whole night? Huh?' She is sipping hot tea and after every sip she jots down something on her notepad.

'We talked about...her trips and clothes and cosmetics.'

'And?' she prompts.

'That's all, I swear.' I am hysterical. 'Why do you keep asking me questions? I know nothing about how she died. I loved her, I loved her like my sister.' I am sobbing now.

~

'Percy, I am so lonely, so alone. I have no family except an old granny who lives in a village and who is almost senile. Percy, I swear to God I know nothing.'

Percy pats my back and says soothingly, 'I know, child, I know.'

But he looks so drawn and haggard. I look at him from the corner of my eye.

In the night Ginny Kalra sails into my room. Her ankles still crossed, her arms still crossed, her throat still slit.

I have terrible nightmares. I go to Dr Pareek. He is old and corrupt. Every time on the pretext of examining me, he squeezes me, takes my flesh between his two fingers and pinches hard, girl, you are too skinny, eat and be merry.

I tell him, I can't sleep, doctor. My migraines are horrible. Give me something to soothe, something to sleep. He prescribes Alprax, as always.

Don't take too many, he leers. I duck and get out.

~

Ginny always smelled so sweet. Ginny, I loved you, loved you so much. Ginny was not my Facebook friend. She was my real friend. She would share her menstrual cramps, the acne on her chin, the hair in her underarms, the dandruff in her ears. She would share her panic attacks, her diarrhoea after eating prawns, her sleep disorders. But she didn't share her boyfriend with me. No, not a hint. Ginny, why did you need a boyfriend when you have me, Ginny, Ginny.

I am bathed in sweat. I must have been screaming and hollering because Bali looks at me aghast from the couch where she has snuggled to sleep.

Someone calls me up in the morning.

We want to do an interview.

I have nothing to say, I stutter into the phone.

It is a man's voice, very earnest and very insistent.

Just a cup of coffee in CCD.

We meet. He is a tall, bearded guy.

Over a cup of hazelnut latte, he asks me if I had known Ginny Kalra for long. He asks tiny harmless questions. Whether I like dark chocolate and who is my favourite actor and who was Ginny's and where we went shopping and who was in her family and then when the coffee is done he says almost inaudibly, 'But Ginny Kalra was into drugs, no?'

'What?' I exclaim.

'You know these high pressure high-flying jobs? Erratic hours, international trips, sleepless nights?'

'Not that I know of,' I retaliate.

'And boyfriends? Or one?'

'No, she didn't tell me all that. Ever.'

I am getting uncomfortable. I have to go. I start getting up. He suddenly proffers a photo.

'Is that the boyfriend?'

I have not ever seen this guy. I gather my bags and leave.

Then it is a floodgate. Phone calls every day. Reporters asking weird questions.

The TV channel GT NOW runs a programme that night,'Friend admits Ginny Kalra was on drugs'. There is a byte of me gaping squint-eyed into the camera, mouthing, 'Drugs? Boyfriend?'

They have edited and put together a collage.

And suddenly after two days there is breaking news.

The postmortem report reveals Ginny Kalra was two months pregnant.

Mrs Delnaz is wringing her hands, whoever thought...

I am sitting in their house. Shireen is holding my hands.

She never confided in me...I am aghast. I thought I knew everything about her.

Ginny's father calls me. He sounds disturbed and upset. He had come alone for Ginny's funeral. Ginny's mother is dead. He lives in the hills with his second wife. A retired army man. Still straight and proud. Now lost and not knowing what had hit him. I had held his hands then, been with him. He had returned after a week. I had gone to see him off at the airport. He had shaken my hands very formally, then had put on his dark glasses and walked through the glass doors, never looking back once. An old bent man devastated at the cruel way his child had died.

Now he calls me.

'Why are they raking up all this muck? It's done, over. She won't come back.'

He sounds bewildered. It's been a fortnight. I have rejoined work. People at my office look at me expectantly. They want all the juicy tidbits. I am the peephole through which they see the sensational murder up close, vicariously.

It is Saturday when Jamset comes running to me.

They have arrested Percy. His words fall over each other. I run downstairs. Mrs Delnaz has had an attack of nerves and taken to her bed. Shireen is crying hysterically.

Next day all of it is in the papers. Percy is the missing link. The boyfriend who has murdered Ginny. Slit her throat and stabbed her in her stomach.

My nightmares return.

Mrs Mudgaonkar is extremely sanctimonious when I see her in her balcony. I can see her kitchen from my kitchen window. Also a bit of the living room. And the tiny utility balcony next to the bathroom looks straight into hers. She is there, hanging out her laundry. She talks to me across the wall that separates us.

'I knew that Percy was a bad apple. Even though I have known him since he was a child. Always thought there was something not right. Too good-looking, too brilliant. Everything a bit too much.'

'Don't say that, Mrs Mudgaonkar. I can't believe it's true,' I retaliate and feel an anger eddying out. I hurriedly remove myself from the balcony.

Mrs Delnaz is in a bad way. Percy's face splashes out from every news channel hungry to create a sensation.

Little by little the pieces fit. I go and meet Percy with Jamset and Shireen. I meet Inspector Ruby Ghorpade. She is tight-lipped. I argue with her.

'At one point you thought I had murdered her? And you were wrong, weren't you?'

She looks at me speculatively. 'You are still on my suspect list,' she says.

'Percy cannot kill.'

'You do not know anything, dear Elena D'souza.'

We are back. In the night I think of all that Percy told me.

That he had flown to Brussels on a business trip. That Ginny Kalra was air hostessing the flight. That in Brussels they had a night together before she flew to New York. That it was just a situational thing. Two people who knew each other thrown together in a strange unknown land. That they met may be twice after that. Still tentative and awkward with each other. Still not intimate with each other, but surely wanting to be.

It seems that night after I left her flat, Ginny had messaged Percy to come up.

I meet Inspector Ruby Ghorpade accidentally in the shopping mall. She is wearing a printed salwar kurta. I agree to have coffee with her. She seems friendlier out of uniform.

She tells me, 'After you left her, Percy went up.

Ginny had called him. We got her mobile details. That's how we zeroed in on Percy. Apparently he went up. They had a lover's tiff. Most likely about the pregnancy, and in a fit of anger, he stabbed her.'

Percy told me he was fast asleep. He never saw her message in the night. It was only in the morning after all the hullaballoo that he checked his phone messages.

She was already dead then.

It's been a month now. The lawyers do not give any hope. Bali looks at me from the windowsill.

Bali, tell me what happened that night? Bali purrs. I have a key to Ginny's flat. A spare key she had given to me for safekeeping. There is another with Mrs Mudgaonkar, Ginny had told me. She had locked herself out once and so as a precaution had distributed her keys.

On an impulse I take out the key from the bedside drawer and go to her flat. The house is empty. I touch her stuff. Her books and tiny knick-knacks, her dressing table, her cosmetics. Everything is as it is. She smiles impishly from the black and white picture on the wall. I sit down on the stool and cry. I miss her so much. And I want to hate Percy but I can't. I can't see him as a jealous lover stabbing Ginny repeatedly.

There is a sound near the window. A pigeon maybe. The window latch was always a bit loose. I get up to close it tightly. As I pull the latch I look out and see a shadow in the opposite flat. Someone moving.

Who is it? The mysterious tenant?

I hurry out and ring the bell. There is silence.

Nothing. I could not have imagined it. I am sure I saw someone.

~

I go to my granny's for a week. I have lost my appetite and she is trying to feed me up. She knows nothing of what I am going through. This is a smalltown place, almost a village. I feel so restless that I cut short my trip and get back home.

As I am trying to open the lock of my flat, I see Arun Mudgaonkar. He is the Mudgaonkars' son. Comes here very rarely and that too for very short visits. I think in the past six months this is his first visit. We nod at each other.

Unpleasant business, this Kalra murder, he mumbles as he goes down the staircase. I don't like him. He looks too flashy, too pompous. I remember Ginny sometimes making fun of him.

I feel emotionally drained and cannot fathom what Mrs Delnaz and Shireen must be going through, for that matter what Percy must be going through. In the evening I go downstairs. Mrs Delnaz and Shireen have gone to the doctor's. Jamset is alone. We sit quietly without speaking.

We have begun to spend quiet evenings like this. All of us just sit together. Sometimes Mrs Delnaz makes tea. Sometimes someone switches on the radio. Mrs Delnaz's brother is coming from abroad to help out with the case.

Mrs Delnaz tells Jamset softly, 'Get the flat cleaned.'

I am talking to Shireen. I hear her but do not register what she is saying. Saturday morning I find Jamset on my landing. The door to the flat next to mine is ajar.

Why? I peep inside.

It is Jamset.

'What are you doing, boy?'

'This is Uncle Dorabji's flat. I am getting it spruced up.'

I am completely astonished. I never knew.

Jamset looks at me slyly, 'Sometimes I come here.'

'Oh, so you were the one I heard moving about...'

I start laughing. Sometimes I actually thought there was some ghostly business going about...

I sit on the chair for some time, then go back to my flat. In the night I can't sleep. I don't want to take Alprax. My temples are throbbing. I take out a Suminat for my migraine but keep it on the bedside table. The pain hammers a nail in my eye and suddenly something flashes in my head. A lightning thought.

~

Uncle Dorabji is a huge giant of a man. Very kindly, and immediately takes everything under control. I can see the difference in Mrs Delnaz and Shireen. It is as if a burden is lifted. I go with Uncle Dorabji to meet Percy. He looks so wasted and haggard. And so resigned.

Something flashes in his eyes. 'Aren't I paying too heavy a price for one night in the sack? Ginny was a great girl but we were not even in love. Why would I kill her?'

He looks as if the bewilderment has hit him like a ten-ton truck. 'It's all a bad dream and I just have to wake up. That's all.'

My heart bleeds for him. I believe him totally.

I call Jamset up to my flat in the evening.

'Do you believe Percy is innocent?'

Jamset looks stricken. He looks away.

I am astonished. 'Why? Do you think Percy has committed this murder? Why Jamset?'

He just gets up and leaves.

After two days when I come back from office he is waiting for me on my landing.

I let him in. I make two cups of coffee and wait for him to unburden himself. Half the coffee is finished before he opens up.

That night he was not able to sleep. So, like many other times he took the key and came upstairs. He read for a while, then fell asleep till a sound woke him up. That was me trying to unlock my flat. After I went in he stayed awake. Went into the kitchen to drink a glass of water. As he filled up his glass in the dark, the moonlight streaming in through the window, he saw a movement in Ginny's flat. He came back to the living room. Next to the door there was a window that opened into the landing. Must have been around four when he heard another sound. As he walked up to the window and peered out, he saw someone going down the stairs hurriedly, just a flash. Not thinking too much about it he had gone downstairs to his flat after some time.

Later when Percy got arrested, he concluded that it was Percy who was fleeing from Ginny's flat in the wee hours.

'I have told no one about it. Not even the police.'

He is trembling now and I hold him in a tight embrace murmuring soothingly, over and over again, 'Everything will be all right.'

But nothing will be all right. How can it be? Was I wrong about Percy? Has he really killed Ginny, my beloved Ginny? Ginny, why did you keep all those secrets from me? If only you had told me everything, everything.

I go to the police station. I hand over Ginny's key to Inspector Ghorpade. She had given it to me for safekeeping, I tell her.

It has been almost six months now. I am trying to forget Ginny. I am trying to get on with my life. Mrs Delnaz is not well. Almost bedridden. Uncle Dorabji has gone back. How much longer can anyone stay like this? Shireen is the surprise package. So strong and so courageous. I admire her. She is holding the house together. People in the society are also trying to fade out the memory. The brief flare of notoriety is fading away. Jamset still comes up sometimes. When he is there, we tap on the walls and I am comforted that he is next door.

Inspector Ruby Ghorpade calls me one day.

'Can you meet me?'

I would rather not if it is not essential. I am distancing myself from this whole business.

This time I get the news from the news channel. There is a press conference by the police. The DIG and other senior police officials. I see Inspector Ruby too.

They are releasing Percy. I can't believe it. I run downstairs. Shireen hugs me. She is crying and laughing, both at the same time.

The forensic labs have given their report. The flesh and blood in Ginny's nails are not Percy's. There was no scratch mark on his body.

It is still a week before Percy can come home. All the formalities are done. Uncle Dorabji has come back. It is festivity time. But till the real murderer is found Percy still walks under a cloud. Jamset and I have still not talked to anyone about the person fleeing down the stairs in the morning. We have still not cleared Percy hundred per cent in our hearts.

The investigation has been reopened. Inspector Ruby Ghorpade has started questioning everyone in the society once again.

We are sitting in my flat one day. She looks pensive. Her plump face has lines of fatigue etched on it. This case is taking its toll on her. But she has caught on to something.

'Let me recreate the scene now. Let's call this man Mr X. He and Ginny are in some sort of relationship but it has gone sour in the past six months. He calls her, she mostly doesn't respond. When she responds, it is only briefly. On that fateful day he calls her. She is vehement about not entertaining him. They have a

fight. He is in another city. He decides to come over.
He travels in the night. Reaches here in the wee hours.
He has a key. Lets himself in. This happens after you
have left. She is caught unawares by his sudden arrival.
They fight again. She tells him about her pregnancy.
Tells him about Percy. Mocks him. He loses his cool.
Is enraged and in a fit of murderous anger, picks up
the scissors and stabs her repeatedly on her throat and
stomach. She starts bleeding profusely. In a panic he
carries her into the bathroom. Dumps her in the tub.
Cleans up a bit and then in a mad panic, leaves in
a hurry. Takes the staircase, there is a bloodstain on
the second landing. He leaves the block through the
small gate that opens into the alley. No one has seen
him. Takes a taxi and travels back to his city. When
the news of the murder breaks he is back in town,
his alibi strong, calls his office and tells them he is at
home with an upset stomach, joins office next day. No
one has any clue that he has travelled three hundred
kilometres to another city.'

She stops.

'Well?'

So it was not Percy but this other guy that Jamset
saw. I decide to finally tell her Jamset's story.

'I wish you had told me earlier. Percy would not
have suffered, maybe.'

'But we thought it was Percy. You would have
thought so too.'

'Maybe yes, maybe no.'

~

We are having dinner at the posh restaurant, Urban Creek. The whole family and me. Percy has begun to perk up slowly. Aunty Delnaz keeps reaching out to touch him. As if he will disappear. I smile and feel happy. Happy for the first time since Ginny went. It was a very bad business but this is life. We have to forget and move ahead. I touch Percy's hands. He looks at me and smiles his calm smile. His smile says, don't worry, I will be fine. I will not let this thing scar me.

He punches Jamset playfully. We have told him how he tried to protect Percy.

It is the support that counts. Family that counts. Shireen glows.

We have all been very brave.

But who would have thought Arun Mudgaonkar held such a grudge against Percy?

It was true, Percy always beat him at everything. In studies and in sports, in jobs and in looks. And finally, he couldn't take it that even Ginny preferred Percy over him. That would have enraged him.

But how did Inspector Ruby get on to him?

She had to go to Ginny's flat that day. She forgot the key and asked the society office for the duplicate key. They told her that the duplicate was with Mrs Mudgaonkar. She went to their flat. Arun was there, he had come a day earlier. When she asked for the key, she caught Arun's alarmed expression in the mirror. Mrs Mudgaonkar couldn't find the key. It was Arun's expression that alerted her. Plus the fact that he was based in Pune. She remembered the call logs from Ginny's mobile. So many calls from Pune. Arun was taken in for questioning, and confessed. Later, the key was found in his Pune flat. He had taken it from his mother's almirah drawer. He had been after Ginny for so long. Pestering and stalking her and in the end he couldn't take it that it was Percy whom she loved.

Poor Mrs Mudgaonkar.

Poor Ginny Kalra.

I am wearing the rust scarf that Ginny had brought for me. A life snuffed too soon, too unfortunately.

Ginny Kalra, I loved you nevertheless.

As we laugh over something inconsequential, Percy and I, the ice cream melts and the cherry on top is blood red on the white vanilla. Outside the sea breeze has begun to blow softly and the smell of the sea rides alongside.

We are trying to forget death. We are laughing too hard, trying too hard to be merry. Death is being postponed for a while.

Ginny, come to me in my dreams.

I cross my fingers under the table and mouth a silent prayer for her. Our Father who art in heaven.

SISTER

Venita Coelho

Sister hated blood. It stank. The thick coppery stink mingled with the smell of incense and sweating people and thickened the air, till it was impossible to breathe.

The goat spasmed as blood gushed and spurted from its neck. The head of the goat had rolled away and it lay watching its own death, with eyes that slowly turned to stone.

Sister hated blood, but it had to be done. She stepped forward and felt the hot blood being pressed between her brows in the spot where the third eye opened.

The most powerful took first blood. Five years ago, Sister had stepped forward first and no one had stood up to challenge her.

The priest dipped both hands in the blood and smeared his face and torso. A roar went up from the crowd and they began to press forward, eager to be anointed.

Sister stepped back, noting with distaste that the

*hem of her sari was soaked in blood. Her eyes were
alert, watching the crowd. If there was any trouble
she and her boys would take care of it. The temple
was tiny and the fervent crowd spilled into the lane
outside. One year there had nearly been a stampede,
but she had climbed on the statue of Kali and shouted
directions and her boys had herded the panic-stricken
crowd to safety like goats.*

*The bells rang, the drums played and the smell of
hot blood hung thick in the tiny space. The mess would
lie in the temple, rank and stinking, until dawn, when
the faithful would return to scrub it from the stones.
The black granite statue of Kali watched it all with a
shocked gaze, eyes wide open to take in all the world.*

*Only Kali was watching as a second sacrifice was
made that night.*

*When the priest unlocked the temple in the pale
light of morning, a boy lay in the blood at Kali's feet.
His arms were stretched above his torso as if he was
prostrating himself before the statue. His head lay
beside him, turned away, eyes closed, as if it hadn't
been able to bear to watch his death.*

~

Inspector T Rakesh stood at the door of the temple
and stared gloomily through the door. Stepping into
it meant stepping into three-inch-deep blood that had
curdled and clotted. He'd never get it off his shoes.
Around him he could hear the other policemen cursing
and retching. It was noon, the sun was strong, and

the small temple must be reeking. For the first time, he was grateful for the cold that had made his life a misery for the last few days. He could smell nothing.

Sighing and resigning himself to a pair of new shoes, he stepped into the temple. He squelched his way to where the body lay, the blood stickily sucking at his shoes. For the umpteenth time he wondered why he hadn't become an accountant.

The body lay prostrated before the statue of Kali. Flies were crawling around the ragged raw wound that was the neck. The head had been hacked uncleanly from the shoulders. The weapon lay on the ground, black with flies. It was an axe. The same that the priest had swung with such skill to behead the sacrificial goat.

The priest stood impassively in the background. He was a large silent man called Laalji. When Inspector Rakesh pointed out that it was his axe that had been used on the boy, he shrugged and said, 'If I had killed him it would have been a clean cut.' He insisted the temple had been empty when he locked up before leaving and he had never seen the boy before. Then he went back to being silent, staring blankly at the Inspector as he asked more questions.

Stepping carefully on the congealed floor and holding down a strong urge to vomit, Rakesh went over to look at the head. It was a young boy, hair tousled, eyes closed. A silver ring pierced an eyebrow. He straightened up, puzzled. 'I've seen that face before,' he said.

Though he wracked his brains about where he could have seen the boy, it was not until they opened the peti that he realized who the boy was. The donation box sat at the feet of Kali. The priest produced a key and opened it. It was filled to the brim with crumpled notes. Collection was always good on the sacrifice day. Half buried in the cash, there was also a wallet and a credit card holder.

'Oh shit!' said Inspector Rakesh when he saw the name on the credit cards. Prem Jindal. He realized why the boy looked familiar. He had seen him often enough on Page Three.

~

'The Jindal heir sacrificed in a small temple in a slum?' The Chief of Police was yelling so loudly, Inspector Rakesh had to hold the phone away from his ear.

'Yes, sir,' said Inspector Rakesh, trying to hold back a sneeze.

'He had his head cut off? Right off?'

'Yes, sir.' Inspector Rakesh tried not to let his nose drip as he fumbled without much hope for a handkerchief.

'Close that slum down! I don't want a single press person in there! They'll be all over this like flies on shit. You need Sister. This is her slum. Ask for Sister,' bellowed the Chief of Police.

'Whose sister?'

'Just ask for her!'

'Ask who?'

'Anyone!' The Chief disconnected.

Inspector Rakesh went hesitantly to the tea stall that leaned against the wall of the temple. A wrinkled old man was brewing a dekchi full of mahogany swill. 'Er—' he began hesitantly. 'I need Sister.'

The man nodded. 'I'll send for her.' He roused his assistant with a clip on the ear and sent him off. The boy wormed his way through the crowd that was being held back by the police.

The Inspector sat on a rickety bench and waited, wishing his cold would go away. Wishing the damn case would go away. Around him policemen held back the crowd as they waited for the official photographer to turn up. The tea stall owner handed him a glass and said, 'Drink, Sahib. It'll take the taste of that place off your tongue and mind.' The tea was strong enough to wipe out entire decades of memory.

The slum lay right beside Bandra Kurla junction and many in the slum made a living from pilfering goods from the trains. A hundred other trades flourished in the slum off the leavings of the city that were digested here. Plastic, trash, building waste, all found its way to the slum and was recycled in a hundred different ways. Three thousand people lived clotted together in the narrow wedge of land between the railway junction and an industrial estate. To Inspector Rakesh's slightly fevered gaze it seemed like every single one of them was crowded into the lane at that moment.

His eye was taken by a flash of white in the crowd.

Nobody ever wore white in a slum. Nobody had the time to put in the effort it took to keep clothes white. The flash resolved itself into a woman in a white sari. She was a head taller than most of the crowd. The crowd itself parted to give her way. She walked slowly and gracefully towards the Inspector, acknowledging the greetings that were called out on every side. Behind her came three young boys. She came up to where Inspector Rakesh sat and greeted him with an inclination of the head. 'You asked for me?'

Inspector Rakesh stared at her. Sister was a eunuch. Quite easily the largest one that he had ever seen. She was six feet tall, lean but well-muscled, impeccably dressed in a crisp white sari. She wore her sari the way the Kohli fisherwomen wore it, swung between the legs and neatly tucked in, so it did not hamper movement. She exuded competence and an edge of menace. But when she spoke it was in a surprisingly gentle voice. There was a smile lurking in her eyes, as if she'd seen that incredulous reaction many times before.

Inspector Rakesh blurted the first thing that came to his mind. 'I bet no one messes with you.'

The smile reached Sister's lips. 'Not for many years—no.'

The Inspector conveyed the request from the Chief of Police. Sister nodded. 'No press people will be allowed in.' She turned to her boys and issued instructions in a low voice. Two of them hurried off through the crowd.

'Do you need any other help?'

Inspector Rakesh was about to say no, when he sneezed enormously instead. Sister reached inside her blouse and produced a crisp white handkerchief and handed it over. The Inspector took it gratefully.

'Show me,' said Sister in a soft voice that brooked no refusal.

~

Sister bent over the body. 'I know the boy,' she said.

'He is a very rich man's son. A businessman.'

Sister nodded. 'He is the boy who was in love with Item.'

'Who?' Inspector Rakesh asked. 'Which item?'

'Item is a dancer at the Night Queen bar. He has been coming here for about two months to see her dance.'

'Who would want him dead?'

'Not Item. She was in love with him.'

'No money was taken. So, who does the death benefit?'

'At the moment, no one but Kali,' said Sister. Inspector Rakesh liked the ironic gleam in her eye. Sister was no fool. Inspector Rakesh considered Sister. She looked back, weighing him up as openly. 'What do you think?' he asked.

'I think that I do not like a murder in my area, one that I had no hint of while it was in the making. I think that I would like very much to know who did it.' She spoke softly and courteously but there was no missing the menace in the voice. Inspector Rakesh wasn't clear what Sister did to those who incurred her displeasure, but he could bet it was nothing pleasant.

'So,' said Sister, leaning forward, 'perhaps I can help? Unofficially.'

'Only if you had nothing to do with the murder.'

'Such drama. A sacrifice for Kali awash with blood. It is not my style, sahib,' said Sister, smiling. 'I assure you. If I wanted someone dead they would die and no one would know.'

Rakesh believed her. He felt a sneeze crawl up his nose. He blew his nose on the borrowed handkerchief hard enough to clear it and immediately regretted the action as the stink in the temple swarmed into his brain.

'Perhaps I should take you to see Item?' said Sister. Inspector Rakesh hastily and gratefully agreed.

~

They walked through the slum, feeling the eyes of the inhabitants thick on them on every side. There were schisms and rifts and strange alliances in the slum. Sister knew the warp and weft of each one and how exactly it made the weave of peace in the place. Whenever a skein trembled, Sister was there creating a patchwork peace, talking to antagonists, brokering deals, getting the slum to carry on. She was good at her work. There had been no riot in the slum since she took over.

On every side people acknowledged her as she passed. The Inspector trailed in her wake, understanding that having Sister on his side was his best chance of getting cooperation and cracking this case. 'How did the kid end up in the slum?' he asked.

'Many of the rich kids come to drink at Night Queen bar. Ever since the ban on dance girls, it's one of the few places where you can still see them. And the rich kids are jaded with normal thrills. They want to do the forbidden. Item was the star of that bar.' Sister shrugged. 'She was sixteen. He was seventeen. These things happen.'

The Night Queen was an ageing dowager in the light of the morning, neon sign hanging askew, garish paint peeling. The bar was on the ground floor and a balcony ran the length of the first floor. It was crowded with women. News of the new sensation had spread fast and all the girls were awake and chattering. There was a flurry of excitement and chatter at the sight of the Inspector. Necks craned, greetings were shouted at Sister. She raised her hands in a graceful namaste, then called up to the girls.

'Did Item's boyfriend come last night?'

'Yes!' called back a woman who seemed to be wearing nothing but a tee-shirt and some smudged lipstick. 'But he left early. Got a phone call and took off.'

'In any case, he's no use when Item isn't there,' added another girl. 'Doesn't spend a rupee.'

'Item wasn't there?'

'Sick,' said another woman in a red nylon negligee. 'What she has to be sick about I don't know. She lives like a bloody princess.'

While this exchange was on, several of the women were discussing the Inspector and his looks. The discussion was audible enough to reach the Inspector and Sister standing below the balcony. The Inspector could feel his ears burning as he ignored the speculations about men in uniform.

Sister asked, 'Is Meena there?'

Meena turned out to be a voluptuous woman dressed in nothing but a sari blouse and a petticoat. She answered their questions seated in one of the deserted booths inside the Night Queen bar.

'Item kept saying that he was going to marry her.' She shrugged, 'Who knows? He came here often enough. But boys like him don't marry bar dancers.'

'Could someone have killed him out of anger?'

Meena gave a laugh. 'Anyone of us. God, we were sick of it!' she mimicked a high pitched voice—'When I'm married, I'll have my own car. When I'm married, I'll bathe in a tub. When I'm married, I'll have servants. She said that the boy was going to buy out Sethna.'

Her voice was poisonous. 'Bad enough Sethna spoilt her rotten. She was sixteen. No talk of her nath being sold. Oh, she was special. She was going to get a husband instead.'

'Who is Sethna?' asked Inspector Rakesh. The girl turned to him and smiled. 'He is our—Mamaji.' The Inspector had known many such Mamaji's in his time.

'Is Item here? We need to talk to her.'

Meena laughed again. 'Her highness doesn't live here. She lives with Sethna. He calls her his adopted daughter. Her mother must have been a very special whore.'

'We should send for this Sethna as well,' said Inspector Rakesh.

Meena burst into a merry laugh. 'You could, but he could not come.'

'I will take you to them,' said Sister.

Sister led him from the Night Queen bar and he followed her long stride, quite mystified.

~

Sethna's house was a double-storeyed brick structure that stood with its grey shoulders above the gay patchwork of plastic and tin all around it. They knocked and a wizened old lady opened the door. She rattled off a burst of Tamil at Sister. Sister replied in calm measured tones. The old lady disappeared through the door. 'You know Tamil?' said the Inspector.

Sister smiled. 'I know all the languages that are spoken in the slum.' The Inspector was taken aback. The slum was awash in people from across India. How many languages did that make?

'Speaking to them in their own language is what has helped me make them into one family,' said Sister.

The old lady returned. The Inspector started for the door, but Sister laid an arm on his, holding him back. The old lady came forward and leaned close to the Inspector. She began to methodically sniff him.

'What...?' said the Inspector, bewildered.

'Sethna is very allergic. Even a strong scent can

set his breathing problems off. The old lady is his smell detector.'

The Inspector was acutely aware that his uniform was synthetic, that he had been walking around sweating in the sun, and his shoes were covered with gore. The old lady made a face and pointed to his shoes. The Inspector removed them and stepped inside barefoot.

The first thing that hit the Inspector as they stepped into Sethna's room was the smell of disinfectant. A row of oxygen tanks stood against one wall. Taking up almost all the space in the room was an enormous bed, reinforced with steel. Lying on it, like a gigantic island, was a man who had to be the fattest that the Inspector had ever seen. His lower body was covered with a sheet. The upper body lay uncovered and flesh overflowed and hung pendulant from every inch. The huge piling and pooling of flesh almost made Inspector Rakesh wince.

They had arrived in the middle of his daily bath. An old woman, who could have been the twin of the one who opened the door, was scrubbing him down, lifting his enormous folds of flab to reach the crevices. The Inspector started as a sudden wail sounded through the house.

'It is my poor girl,' said Sethna. 'Her heart is quite broken. First love. It can leave you devastated.' His flaps of flat wobbled and shook as the old woman wiped firmly.

'You see before you a broken man. Broken,' said Sethna. 'That boy was going to change my life.'

'So, negotiations had been concluded satisfactorily?' asked Sister.

Sethna shot a quick look at the Inspector. 'He meant to marry her. He was most generous in calculating compensation for—ah, the sums I had spent on Item's upkeep all these years.'

'And now he is gone. Such is life,' said Sister. 'Who could have wanted him dead?'

'Surely you don't suspect me?' said Sethna. 'I most certainly wanted him alive. As did Item. What good is a dead groom, however rich he is?'

'So, who do you think did it?' asked Sister. There was a pause as the woman flung a white sheet over the vast bulk of Sethna, and left the room.

Sethna sank back in his pillows. 'I think there are only two motives for murder—love and money.'

'Hate,' said Sister, suggesting a third, but Sethna was having none of it.

'That is only another face of love. So, if I were you I would look at the money. Rather a lot of it in this case. And I would look at love.'

'Was someone else in love with Item?'

Sethna began to chuckle. It made all his flesh wobble and his enormous bed tremble. 'Rather a lot of them. Half the slum. Everyone over nine and under ninety. Oh, the trouble I've had with suitors.' He leaned forward and waved one fat finger. 'But I was most careful with my girl. She is pure. Untouched.'

'And no doubt you will find someone else to compensate you handsomely for—bringing her up,' said the Inspector with irony. 'I should point out that we will be keeping an eye on the girl.'

'Of course,' said Sethna. 'I have great faith in the law. I am sure you will solve the murder.' But as he lay there, all his flesh rippled with the effort of holding back laughter.

'You know something,' said Inspector Rakesh, 'don't make me take it out of you.'

'Oh, please do,' said Sethna smiling insolently up at the Inspector. 'It would be such a relief to shed something.'

The moment of challenge was broken by one of the old women who came running through the door. She rattled off a string of frantic Tamil.

'It is Item,' said Sister. 'She is on the roof and refusing to come down. They are afraid she might jump.'

'Save my poor girl!' begged Sethna.

~

The roof was tiny and lined with water tanks. Pigeons fluttered everywhere. A moving, shifting floor of pigeons lay between them and where Item stood at the edge of the terrace. She was red-eyed from crying. Her kajal had smeared and her nail polish was chipped. Cheaply dressed and ravaged by grief she was still a very beautiful girl. Only at sixteen could you cry all day and still look beautiful.

Sister gestured for them to stay back as she walked towards Item. Item was screaming, 'He was going to marry me! He was going to take me away from here. They killed him to stop him. I hate them!'

'Who are they, child?' asked Sister gently.

The bitter tears grated out of Item's eyes with difficulty. 'His mother, the bitch. She didn't want him to marry me. He told me.'

'Can you really blame her child?' said Sister, slowly edging forward.

'Why?' said Item fiercely. 'Am I not smart? Beautiful? And I'm untouched. It's not my fault I was born here. It's not fair not to give a person even one chance!'

'Life knows nothing of fairness,' said Sister. She had learnt that when she was nine years old and had been snatched from her family. At twelve when they had put her under the knife, she had given up dreaming that she would find her way back home one day. And she learnt soon enough that the only fairness was that which you made yourself.

'He's dead!' Item wailed. 'I loved him and he's dead!' She held out one despairing hand. Long ropes of blood were crawling down it.

'She's cut her wrists!' said Sister, covering the space between them in one swift movement and grabbing Item.

~

Sister carried Item down to a room on the first floor. She cut off the bleeding and snapped orders for bandages. The old lady hurried off while Sethna yelled anxious queries from downstairs. 'Is she dead? Tell me—is my darling girl dead?'

'Shall I call an ambulance?' asked Inspector Rakesh.

'No,' said Sister. 'Sethna will never allow her to leave. I will take care of this. I am a healer.' Sister bandaged efficiently. Then she put her arms around Item and held the girl close.

'I don't want to live,' sobbed Item. 'I don't want to live! He's gone. She killed him.'

'Who killed him?' asked the Inspector. Item turned her swollen eyes to him and spat the words. 'I already told you. His mother!

'His birthday was just two months away. He was going to marry me on his birthday. It was the day that all the money came to him and she got nothing. So she killed him! The bitch! And now you won't let me die. You won't let me die!'

Sister tucked Item into bed as the girl sobbed hopelessly. 'Who will I live for? He is gone!'

'You will find something,' said Sister, softly. 'We all do.'

She held the girl's hand until her sobs quietened and she fell into a troubled sleep.

The Inspector's phone rang. It was the Chief and he was not happy. 'What the hell are you still doing there? Get back to office. Now!'

～

The usual bedlam reigned at the station. Everyone sitting in the office was soaked in sweat. It was filthy hot and the station was crowded, the air stirred fitfully by ancient fans. Inspector Rakesh stepped into the Chief's room and gave a sigh of relief as the coolness of air conditioning settled around him.

A woman was sitting across the table from the Chief. She was dressed all in spotless white and an enormous pair of dark glasses masked almost all of her face. 'Ah—here is the officer in charge of the case,' said the Chief. 'Meet Mrs Jindal.'

'It can't be true,' said Mrs Jindal in a husky voice. 'It can't be my son.'

'I am afraid it is,' said Inspector Rakesh.

'Who did this to him?' said Mrs Jindal, rising to her feet. She was very tiny, barely coming up to the Inspector's shoulder, even in her fancy high heels. 'Find them, officer! Find them and punish them! I have only one son.'

'Er—I had a few questions,' said Inspector Rakesh. 'I wanted to know about the will your husband left.'

'What?' said Mrs Jindal in surprise. 'You want to know about my husband's will, instead of doing something to catch my son's killers? What kind of an officer are you?'

'Just a few questions madam—'

Mrs Jindal gave a moan and swayed on her feet.

'Rakesh!' The Chief was on his feet. 'You are talking to a lady deep in grief. I am so sorry, madam.'

Mrs Jindal had grabbed her bag. 'I will be talking to the press about this!' she said. 'How I was harassed at a time of grief.'

'Madam—we will do our best to get you justice. I assure you,' said the Chief, but she marched out of the room, leaving such a strong smell of perfume in her wake that it even penetrated Inspector Rakesh's clogged nostrils.

The Chief shrugged. Then he turned to Rakesh. 'You're an idiot, Rakesh. Always politeness in front of them. Never the wrong question. They expect you to lick their asses and you must.'

'Er …' said Inspector Rakesh, but the Chief wasn't finished. 'But only until you get your hands on the proof. Then you arrest the fuckers and put them in jail.' He angled his chair to get the most of the air conditioning. 'Do you know how much she is worth?'

Inspector Rakesh had been busy on Google on the way to the office. 'The net assets of the companies are estimated at 350 crores. However, market evaluation will be affected by the death of the heir. It is estimated to fall between five and seven per cent.'

The Chief regarded Inspector Rakesh with affection. 'I keep forgetting you were almost an accountant. Three hundred and fifty crores. Do you know what the husband left her? A two-bedroom flat and one lakh a month. I don't think that will cover her laundry bill.'

He smiled at Inspector Rakesh's surprised expression. 'Oh yes. I've been working on the case too. Ask me about the will. Who does it all go to?'

'The son. On his eighteenth birthday,' said Inspector Rakesh. 'Which is two months away.'

'So now—get me proof,' said the Inspector.

~

Night never came entirely to the slum. Hidden under the variegated plastic and tin were dozens of smallscale industries that worked all hours. Workers came and went. Scavengers delivered plastic bags of waste to the ever-running sorting mills. Tea stalls and tiny hotels stayed open through the night. The slum even had a gym that was open twenty-four hours. The only time that silence seemed to fall in the slum was between the hours of two and four in the morning. It was in that silence that Sister's phone rang. Item sobbed hysterically at the other end. 'He's dead. Sethna is dead!'

Sister hurried over and one of the old women opened the door. Tears were running down her wrinkled face. Wordlessly, she pointed.

Sethna seemed even more massive in death. He lay bloated and congealed on his bed. His face was purple. The bedclothes were in disarray. He had struggled for every breath.

'Who was here?' Sister said sharply to the two old women. They looked at her with ancient eyes. They had kept Sethna's secrets in life and Sister knew she was unlikely to get them to give them up now. Item's wails carried down from the first floor.

'Touch nothing. See to her. Don't let her harm herself again,' said Sister.

~

Inspector Rakesh arrived rumpled and cranky. He had buttoned his shirt up the wrong way. He stared down at the huge bulk of Sethna.

'Damn. Another corpse.' Moodily, he thought about a transfer to a nice quiet rural posting. Something like Nanded. At least he'd get fresh milk to drink. 'Let's talk to the old women.'

They found the old women busy packing. Sister spoke to them in Tamil telling them they could not leave, the police needed to talk them. Both women looked at her in stubborn silence. A rapid string of words fell from Sister's lips. Inspector Rakesh had no idea what she said. But one of the old women began to talk. Inspector Rakesh waited anxiously for the translation.

'They say they know nothing. Sethna forbade them from coming out of their room between twelve and two. That was the time people visited him for his business. They left the door open and stayed in their own room. They had no idea who visited him.'

'So, anyone could have got in.'

The old lady hesitated, then let off a rattle of Tamil.

'She says when she found him, there was the smell of perfume in the room. The smell of roses. She is the one who smells people. Her nose is never wrong.'

Sister noted Inspector Rakesh's reaction. 'What does that mean to you?'

'Mrs Jindal wears a fancy perfume,' he said. 'I met her today. I think it smelt of roses, though I can't be sure because of my cold.'

Sister looked thoughtfully down at Sethna. 'He was very allergic. The perfume might even have sparked off an asthma attack and killed him.'

'So, one man was killed with an axe, another with perfume? This damn case gets weirder all the time.' A thought struck the Inspector. 'How the hell are we going to get him out of here and to the morgue for a post-mortem? It'll take a truck.'

'And a bulldozer,' said Sister.

~

In the end it took a team of labourers and a JCB. They had to break down the door. Half the slum gathered to watch.

While the JCB manoeuvered in the narrow lane, Sister and the Inspector searched through Sethna's room. Under his enormous bed there were tin trunks filled with yellowing papers and photographs. Some of the photographs were of his 'girls' across the years. Others were of unknown men. There were hundreds of articles clipped from ancient newspapers.

Inspector Rakesh and Sister were leafing through their find when they heard a shout and then a roar of excitement.

They came through the door and looked in astonishment at the sight before them. Bank notes billowed in the air. Great clouds of money swirled and swooped around. In the narrow lane, people jostled and shoved, leaping to grab them. The labourers had smashed through the beam above the door—and into a hidden cache of money that a gust of wind had scattered.

'Stop!' yelled Inspector Rakesh, 'that money is

evidence!' No one took the slightest notice of him as they rioted on every side, money lust upon them.

Sister leapt forward, grabbing a spar of wood from the wreckage. She spun it around her head in circles, shifting it from one hand to the other, stepping into the crowd. The stick cracked against heads, shoulders, grasping hands. There were shrieks as the crowd realized it was Sister. They began to scramble backwards. Sister advanced, the stick dancing around her, tossed from hand to hand, weaving around her body in a dazzling display. It looked like a graceful dance of which Sister was the quiet, balanced centre. But flickering at the edges of the dance was the wooden stick, finely balanced to wreak punishment. The crowd quietened, edged back.

The Inspector had never seen the ancient martial art of Kalaripayatem in action before. It is the discipline that is said to be the mother of all other martial arts. He stood there staring.

Sister moved in ever widening circles, the spar spinning around her, whispering in a wicked whiplash voice. Showers of money fell around her as she spun and whirled. Behind her two sub-inspectors scuttled forward, grabbing money as fast as they could. When the crowd was reduced to hypnotized docility, Sister stopped. She tossed away the stick and walked back to the house without bothering to look over her shoulder.

∼

They put the money they salvaged into a carton. The notes had been torn and crumpled by mass greed. Only two bricks of notes had been left intact in the cache.

'God knows how much that crowd made off with,' said the Inspector.

'We can get fingerprints off these at least,' said Sister, pointing to the untouched bricks of notes. 'How soon do you think you can get them?'

Inspector Rakesh gave her a sardonic look. 'Where do you think you are? In the middle of a crime episode in an American TV series? The lab at Bhayander was flooded during the monsoons and they're still cleaning the equipment. The nearest lab is in Pune but that has a backlog of three months. The fingerprints from the damn axe won't come to us for months. And the Chief is breathing down my neck to close the case as soon as possible.'

The Inspector held up what he had salvaged from the secret cache in the wooden beam. Several tiny notebooks filled with figures.

'What's in them?' asked Sister.

'Sethna's accounts. I think he ran a nice line in blackmail and in here are all those he took money from. Except that it's in some sort of code.'

'How long will that take to work out?'

'Not long,' said Inspector Rakesh, sounding unexpectedly cheerful. He loved accounts and he loved codes.

'Well,' said Sister, holding up the article she had

been reading before the riot. 'Mrs Jindal might be on that blackmail list.'

~

Mrs Jindal had to fight her way to the police station through a feeding frenzy of journalists and cameras. She was spitting like an angry cobra by the time she came through the door. She came with a lawyer in tow. She brought with her a smell. A flowery perfume that jostled with the other smells in the police station. Sister took a deep breath and caught the Inspector's eye meaningfully.

'Why have you called me to the police station?' Mrs Jindal snapped at Inspector Rakesh. 'It had better be for a good reason.'

'We wanted to ask you some questions.'

Mrs Jindal smoothened her hair down and composed herself. 'Me? What about?'

'Did you know someone called Sethna?' said Inspector Rakesh.

'Who?' asked Mrs Jindal.

'He was a pimp in the slum.'

Mrs Jindal gave him an incredulous stare. 'Are you mad? I thought you called me because you knew who had done it. Who had killed my son. Instead you want to know if I know some pimp?'

'We found some articles about you in his house.'

Mrs Jindal went very still. When she spoke it was in soft gentle tones that cut like ice. 'Are you casting the aspersion that I think you are? Careful, Inspector.

I can have you transferred to the back of beyond with one phone call.'

Wearily, the Inspector thought that the back of beyond would come as a welcome relief. The lawyer interrupted.

'Inspector, my client is happy to answer questions relevant to the case.'

'This is relevant,' said the Inspector doggedly. 'Did she know Sethna?'

'You must understand, Inspector, that my client is grieving for her son. This is the time to be understanding, not ask questions.'

Sister spoke up from her seat in the corner. 'That is a beautiful perfume you are wearing.'

Mrs Jindal looked at her like she was crazy. Then she shrugged. 'It is blended especially for me.'

'Where would that be?' asked Inspector Rakesh.

Mrs Jindal got to her feet, 'Have you gone mad? You've called me in to ask me questions about some pimp and my perfume? Are you insane?'

'Please, Mrs Jindal,' began her lawyer soothingly, but she was having nothing of it.

'My son was found dead in a slum. A slum! A place that is full of drugs and dealers and thieves.'

Sister spoke in her gentle voice. 'No, it is not,' she said. 'Not my slum.'

Mrs Jindal swung around to stare at Sister for a moment. 'And eunuchs,' she added with biting scorn. 'Ask them the questions! Any of them could have done this.'

'We found his wallet and credit cards. Nothing had been taken. It was not a robbery.'

'And now your team of incompetents and eunuchs thinks I'm involved?'

Inspector Rakesh gestured for her to sit. 'Your son was in a relationship with a girl called Item.'

'Relationship?' said Mrs Jindal. 'A greedy little thing had her nails in him, Inspector. A mere bar dancer. She led him to his death.'

'Her—ah—protector—was a man called Sethna. Today from Sethna we recovered rather a large sum of money. And a cache of articles and photographs.'

'Isn't it obvious where a pimp gets his money from? From his whore. Ask that girl.'

Sister spoke up softly. 'Item's nath had not yet been taken. She was not his whore but his adopted daughter.'

'What does this have to do with me?' said Mrs Jindal, raising one perfect eyebrow.

'We had the money fingerprinted,' said Sister and sat back to see the result. They had decided that she would be the one to bluff, since Inspector Rakesh was not officially allowed to lie.

There was a moment of dense silence. Then Mrs Jindal said, 'I would like to make a statement.'

It threw her lawyer into a tizzy. 'You don't have to say a thing! I would strongly advise against it.'

'Be quiet!' snapped Mrs Jindal. 'I would like to make a statement.' The lawyer tried to argue with her sotto voce.

She spoke over the agonized whispers of the lawyer. 'I never intended for anyone to be killed. Least of all my son.' Her face crumpled and for the first time the grief shone through. Then she pulled herself together, smoothened her hair, folded her hands and said, 'I'm ready.'

She took a deep breath and spoke in calm tones. 'My husband was bored with me. We had been married far too long. Rich men don't divorce their wives. It's bad for business. But they don't have to leave them anything if they don't feel like it either.'

'Your son got everything,' said Sister.

'Yes,' said Mrs Jindal. 'And I loved him. You think I paid Sethna to kill him? I paid him to stop it. Stop the stupid affair. I found out about it and I went to meet the pimp. I gave him the money and told him to stop it. No one was supposed to die! If you don't believe me, ask Sethna. Ask him what I paid him to do on my behalf.'

The lawyer sat with his head sunk in his hands.

'We would ask him,' said Inspector Rakesh, watching her closely. 'Except the reason he couldn't tell us who gave him the money, is that he is dead.'

Sister watched Mrs Jindal age twenty years in two seconds. Her face sagged. Every line suddenly struggled free of the make-up. She sat there staring at them, a middle-aged lady with the gloss stripped away by shock.

'He's dead?'

'Murdered,' said Inspector Rakesh. 'He choked to

death. He was highly allergic. Perhaps killing him was as simple as a spritz of perfume in the nostrils. The room smelt of perfume. Your perfume.'

'No,' said Mrs Jindal. 'No.' She sagged back in her chair.

Her lawyer did not allow her to say a word after that. 'Get a warrant,' he said. 'No judge in the world will give you a warrant when the only evidence you have is a smell.' He took Mrs Jindal's arm. 'We are leaving.'

In the waiting room outside the lawyer tried to lead her to the door, but Mrs Jindal came to a sudden stop. Item was sitting in a plastic chair, her bandaged wrists in her lap, misery in the droop of her shoulders. 'Is that her?' asked Mrs Jindal abruptly. 'Is that the girl?'

Item looked up. The two women stared at each other, the polished society lady and the garish young girl. Then Item spat at Mrs Jindal. The gobbet landed on one expensive shoe. Mrs Jindal did not move, just held the girl's look. The lawyer broke the moment, grabbing her arm and steering her to the door. They stepped into a wall of shouted questions and flashing lights.

~

Item was not happy. 'It was her! And you let her go! She's behind it all. She killed Sethna too.'

'Did you see anything? Hear anything?'

Item shook her head. 'I was asleep. One of the women woke me. They checked on him every few hours through the night. They went to check—and found him lying dead. I called you.'

'Did Sethna tell you to stop seeing the boy?' said Sister.

Item hesitated. Then she said, 'Yes. He told me to stop. He wouldn't tell me why.' She spoke fiercely. 'I loved Prem. He was going to marry me. So, I made Sethna an offer.'

'An offer?' said Inspector Rakesh.

Item looked at them defiantly. 'I knew it was her. I knew she had offered him money to make me stop seeing her son. Well, once I was married I would be rich and I would give him double. I told him. I swore it. I would have. We would have been rich and she would have had nothing.'

~

The slum was a good place to hide. Sister's boys made sure that none of the press could get into it. Those who managed to sneak in found it impossible to get into Sister's home. Her house was one of the few permanent structures in the slum, a remnant of the fisherman's colony that had once stood in the space. It was built around a courtyard and was shaded by an ancient tree. A small temple stood in one corner of the courtyard, with a tower topped by fantastically carved and painted protector gods. It was a South Indian temple, and the god within had two wives.

Sister was holding class in the tiny courtyard. She taught Kalaripayetam to the girls and the boys of the slum. Five of them were practicing with long sticks, the whisper and whistle of the movement filling the small space. Sister insisted that all the children of the slum be able to defend themselves. Since the philosophy of Kalaripayetam demanded that a practitioner also heal the wounds that he inflicted, the children were also taught to be healers. It was a philosophy that Sister found handy for life as well.

Inspector Rakesh sat at a desk and tried to decipher the code in the little books. The figures he had already sorted out. He had originally planned to be an accountant and his eye for figures was remarkable. Now he was working on Sethna's peculiar personal code. He could not understand what it stood for. From time to time he called questions to Sister, interrupting the clacking of the sticks.

'So, if Item offered him double the money, would Sethna have taken the offer?'

'Yes,' said Sister, without breaking her rhythm. She had little doubt that Sethna always sold to the highest bidder.

'So Mrs Jindal paid for the affair to be ended. Item bribed Sethna to do nothing. Then how the hell did the kid end up as a sacrifice in a temple?'

'We've looked at money as a motive,' said Sister, 'perhaps it's time to look at love.' A flurry of stickwork forced a girl onto the backfoot.

Inspector Rakesh stared down at the figures of the code. With Sister's words he had understood what the code stood for. Sister saw his sudden stillness and came over, wiping sweat from her face.

'Sexual preferences,' said Inspector Rakesh. 'That's what the code records. Sethna kept a log of the sexual preferences of all the clients. That is what he blackmailed them with. Look, it's simple enough. This is—er—homosexuals. And this is—young girls. These are various—er—positions. And here are—' Inspector Rakesh blanched.

'Children,' said Sister. She had been one of the children a long time ago.

Inspector Rakesh got to his feet. 'I hate this case! I hate it. I hate that there are things like this in the world.'

'That is why we must stand against them,' said Sister, softly. She had stood. Children were no longer trafficked in the slum.

Suddenly the Inspector could stand it no longer. All his unhappiness bubbled up. The raw truths that police work showed you every day. The hatred and the cruelty and the never ending darkness of it all. 'I want a transfer,' he said.

Sister grabbed Inspector Rakesh's arm, and her grip was strong. Sister's voice was like a whiplash. 'You will stand!' she said.

~

Laalji, the priest, and Sister were old acquaintances. In the evenings Laalji taught wrestling in the tiny courtyard of the temple. He had never quite forgiven Sister for all the youngsters who defected to learn Kalaripayetam. He opened up the temple and let them in.

Before they stepped in, Sister had a word with Laalji. The priest never said much but little escaped him.

'Who was in love with Item? Everyone,' he said. 'Old Murugesh of the scrap shop. The young mechanic—what's his name—Joshi who works at the garage. The Toda brothers. It was her fault, of course. Walking up and down, shaking her hips, smiling. That girl was a flirt.'

'What was the kid doing in your temple? Ever come here before?'

'No. He didn't come to the slum to pray at a temple.'

'Any ideas?'

The priest shrugged. 'I'll tell you this. Whoever did it was an amateur. It wasn't a nice clean jhatka.'

'But he was strong,' said Sister thoughtfully. 'It takes strength to hack through a neck.'

The temple was a far cry from the first time that Inspector Rakesh stepped into it. It was spotless and smelt of incense. Somebody had hung a garland of fresh hibiscus around Kali's neck. In the light of the day her menacing gaze had reduced to mere wide-eyed curiosity. Inspector Rakesh stood before Kali. 'What are we here for?' he asked Sister.

'We are here to ask for help,' said Sister. She looked up at Kali looming over her and joined her hands. Inspector Rakesh reluctantly joined his hands as well, furtively looking around to make sure that the priest was gone.

'A young boy is dead. His mother genuinely grieves. A young girl genuinely grieves. Surely you—a mother and a woman yourself, want justice done?'

Sister said in low tones. 'Help me, Maa.' Kali gazed back at her with fixed eyes.

'What did you see that night?' asked Sister. 'You know what happened.' The thought stayed with her. Suddenly she grasped one of the arms of the statue and climbed up so that she was peering over Kali's shoulder. What had Kali seen?

From the new perspective Sister saw something that had missed everybody else. Kali's weapons had been liberally bedaubed with red paint. But smeared on a chopper in her right hand was something that didn't quite match.

∼

'But we have blood on Laalji's axe!' wailed Inspector Rakesh, now thoroughly fed up of the case. 'Why is there blood on Kali's weapon?'

'Perhaps Kali killed him,' said Sister.

'Oh, stop it,' said Inspector Rakesh. 'I am putting in for a transfer to Nanded. I've had enough of this damn case. I don't want to hear a thing.'

'Don't say that,' chided Sister. 'Not when I just solved it.'

'You solved it?' asked the Inspector in astounded accents.

'Yes,' said Sister, 'it is simple actually. The boy was killed twice.'

The Inspector thought fervently that if she hadn't been so damn big he would have hit her.

'I think we should gather everyone here,' said Sister. 'I can explain what happened.'

'Gather everyone?'

'All those who could have been the murderers,' said Sister.

'That's not going to happen,' said Inspector Rakesh. 'This is not some English film with a climax.'

Sister smiled. 'I will speak to the Chief.'

'What is it with you and the Chief?' said Inspector Rakesh.

'I have been of help to him before,' said Sister. 'He trusts me. Don't you?'

Inspector Rakesh had to admit that he did.

～

It was a strange group of people that gathered in the temple. The Chief was there. It was only his insistence that had brought Mrs Jindal. She arrived with her lawyer. She had refused to come without him and had said that she would not be speaking at all. Inspector Rakesh had arranged stools for them to sit on.

The two wizened old women from Sethna's household sat in one corner, watching everything with sharp eyes. Item sat on the floor beside them. Her eyes were fixed on Mrs Jindal, burning with the intensity of her hate.

Laalji the priest sat at the feet of Kali, arranging puja items on a plate.

Sister stood facing them, in her trademark spotless white sari. She smiled and joined her hands in greeting.

Mrs Jindal was edgy and uncomfortable. 'Can we please hurry this up? I don't want to be here. Not where my son—' her voice trailed off and choked.

Sister inclined an apologetic head. 'I am sorry. I felt it was important to be here to understand what really happened that night.'

'You know what happened?' asked Mrs Jindal.

'Yes,' said Sister.

'Who are you?' asked Mrs Jindal, looking properly at Sister for the first time.

'They call me Sister,' said Sister simply. 'This is my slum. And I was most unhappy that this incident happened here. So, I assisted the police with their enquiries.'

Mrs Jindal put her head to one side and regarded Sister. Something of Sister's calm surety communicated itself to her. 'I don't like this place. Make it fast,' she said.

'Before Sethna died, he said a curious thing that I now believe to be true. There are only two motives for murder. Love and money. Let's see all that happened in the light of these two,' said Sister.

Everyone waited expectantly. 'Let's start at the beginning. Why did the boy first come to the slum? Did he and his friends come for a few thrills at a bar where girls danced to item numbers? I don't believe in chance. I think that the first time ever Prem Jindal came to this slum he came with a purpose. He was due to inherit a huge amount. The only other contender was his mother. I think perhaps he followed his mother. And she led him here.'

Mrs Jindal's reaction was immediate. 'What on earth would I be doing in a slum? Why would I come here? I've got no connection to all this—pimps and whores and ...' she gave a shudder.

Sister inclined her head. 'Why indeed? In a conversation we had I said to you that Item's nath had not sold yet. You didn't ask me what I meant. You understood perfectly. How did you understand the language of pimps and whores?'

Mrs Jindal didn't miss a beat. 'I must have seen it in a movie. Or on television.'

'Or you were once part of this world,' said Sister softly. 'Your nath was once sold here. At a very high price.' Mrs Jindal opened her mouth to protest but Sister held up a hand. 'It was a photograph among the papers under his bed. Sethna couldn't resist keeping one showing his favourite girl. No one would have recognized you. But I was searching for the link.'

Mrs Jindal stared at Sister.

'Heera,' said Sister softly, 'you danced under the name of Heera.'

~

Heera. She had chosen the name herself. Because a diamond shone even in the dirt. And she was born to shine. She knew it. She wasn't like the other girls. She danced with all her heart. She closed her eyes and danced and dreamed. One day there would be a film producer in the bar. One day her life would change.

She didn't bother with the quiet potbellied man who sat at the far table night after night. She didn't pay him much attention until the showers of money.

Not for him ten-rupee notes. He showered her with hundreds. And one day he bought her a diamond nose ring. A diamond for her name. Heera.

~

Sister looked at the polished expensive lady. Twenty years removed from a raw young bar dancer.

The lawyer began to protest. 'That is a serious allegation! My client—'

His client turned and hissed at him, 'Shut up!' Then she turned back to Sister. 'I am only listening to this insulting nonsense because I want to know who killed my son. Tell me that.'

But Sister was only at the beginning of her story. 'The man who bought your nath also bought you. He paid your full contract and took you away from here. He married you.'

Sister continued almost in a monotone, 'And so we come to love. That was the love story that started it all. The brash young businessman with a bright future and the bar girl.'

~

Nobody wanted to marry bar girls. Least of all men who were going to be rich. But the man who brought her diamonds was in love with her. He was the son of a trucker and he had dreams like she had. He was going to make a fortune on the stock exchange. And he was going to marry her.

She tried to remember that as he breathed hard

through his mouth and pawed her with hands that left bruises. Marriage. Money. A way out of here. This time when she closed her eyes she didn't dream of dancing on the screen. She dreamed of her name on the society pages. Of a room of her own. White. She would only wear white when she got away from all of this. Because only those who don't wash their own clothes wear white all the time.

~

Sister's voice held them all. 'He married you and you became Mrs Jindal. Over time you became rich, a society lady. Far, far removed from where you had begun. But then Sethna fell on hard times. He remembered his star. He had always indulged in petty blackmail. Now he had a really big fish.'

Mrs Jindal said nothing, not even acknowledging that Sister was speaking to her. Sister did not stop. 'You began to pay him. Year after year. I imagine the higher you got on the social ladder, the bigger the premium. The rich and polished society lady Mrs Jindal could not possibly let people know that she started out as a bar dancer.'

Mrs Jindal said nothing. She sat silent, her eyes fixed on Sister. 'And then—disaster. Your son followed you to the slum to see where you were going.'

Mrs Jindal kept her eyes lowered. But she was remembering.

~

Prem. He was named for love. The love wore off fast enough. The richer Jindal got, the more he regretted that he had chosen a bar dancer. Regretted that he had got married at all when he could have any woman that he chose.

Prem had grown up hearing Digvijay and his mother fight and argue. Tormented and torn between the two of them. Wondering what it was that Digvijay flung in his mother's face again and again. He presumed it was an affair.

He was sent away abroad to be kept from his mother's influence, returning only when his father was dead. His mother loved him. She tried to mend things between them again and again. He wouldn't listen. He wouldn't believe that she had nothing to hide. That the heart attack his father died of had nothing to do with her. She could have told him his father died on top of his young mistress. But she kept quiet. And then one night he followed her.

~

'Your son followed you. Stepped into a bar. And saw another young girl dancing. Like his father before him—he fell in love.'

~

A young girl dancing with all her heart. Eyes closed. Dreaming. The most beautiful alive thing he had ever seen. Nothing like the polished girls that he had known so far. Raw, alive with laughter. With wicked teasing eyes and a way of looking at him that drove

*him crazy. Item. What a crazy name for a girl. But
she was an Item all right. And he fell in love with her.*

~

Mrs Jindal sat there, listening with an expressionless
face. Her lawyer was sweating profusely.

Sister continued in her soft voice. 'She was sixteen,
he was seventeen. These things happen.'

From her corner, Item spoke up fiercely. 'He loved
me! He really did.'

'This would be the second time that a rich man fell
in love with a bar dancer,' continued Sister, ignoring
the interrruption. 'But this one wouldn't be allowed
to end in marriage. It was the last thing you would
have wanted for your son, wasn't it?'

Mrs Jindal turned her head away, only to find
herself meeting Item's intense eyes. She dropped her
gaze.

'I think Sethna called you and warned you of
what was happening. But when you confronted your
son, he wouldn't listen. He was in love.' Sister spoke
directly to Mrs Jindal. 'Love or money. Either you
loved your son and was afraid that he would ruin his
life and did everything to stop this disastrous match.
Or money—you were afraid that he would marry the
girl, you would be exposed and you would lose every
paisa, even the paltry inheritance Jindal had left you.'

'I was a good mother,' said Mrs Jindal, her voice
intense. 'I loved my son.'

'The timing was crucial,' said Sister. 'There were

just two more months before he became an adult. Two more months and he would marry her. Just two more months and he would have everything and you would have nothing. Money is a powerful motive.'

Mrs Jindal's voice was a half-sob. 'I didn't have my son killed! I loved him! He was all I had left to love!'

The lawyer shot upright. 'My client will be leaving now—'

'Sit down,' said the Chief, from where he had been sitting listening. 'Nobody leaves till the story is over.'

'I will be filing a complaint! You will be transferred!'

'File away,' said the Chief.

'My client is innocent!'

From the silence in the room it was clear that nobody believed him. Mrs Jindal made no effort to defend herself. She looked at Sister and said wearily,

'Think what you like. I loved my son. I only tried to stop him. I never tried to get him killed.'

'Liar!' spat Item. 'Liar! It was you! You got him killed.'

'Silence!' said Sister and the girl fell quiet. Sister turned to Mrs Jindal. 'Yes. I think that is what you tried to do. You paid Sethna. And you asked him to stop it.'

All eyes were back on Sister. In her white sari, she stood like a counterpoint to the dark figure of Kali. 'Love. Two teenagers in love. When has any parent managed to stop them? Sethna tried, but Item wouldn't listen to him. He was a prisoner of his flesh.

He couldn't get out of the house. Couldn't keep an eye on Item. And Item had grown headstrong and unafraid. Desperate, Sethna enlisted some help.'

Everyone was frozen in place. Even the lawyer was riveted. Sister looked around her and continued, 'And so, at last, we arrive here. On the night of the ceremony. A goat was sacrificed before hundreds of people. But no one was there to see what happened later in the night. No one but Kali.'

~

The sound of Item's anklets at the door of the temple. Their merry sound slowing and clinking to silence as she paused at the threshold, loath to step into the blood.

The man stepped up from behind her in the darkness and grabbed her hair. He bent her backwards. His lips whispered in her ears. Ugly words of what would happen if she did not stop seeing the boy. Of the sacrifice that would be made in the temple. A true sacrifice to Kali.

The girl was terrified. She fell to her knees and begged for her life. She promised that she would break it up. She begged for ten minutes alone with the boy to explain. To make him understand.

~

Item suddenly spoke up, 'He told me he would cut my throat. He said he would make a necklace of my fingers for Kali! He threatened me.' Her finger pointed to where Laalji sat silent at the edge of the group. All eyes turned to him.

Laalji said nothing, sitting there impassive, his eyes going from one woman to the other, as Sister spoke again.

'Sethna called in a man he knew was discreet. And could do what he asked. He was to threaten the girl. And the boy.' Sister turned to Item. 'He let you make a phone call. You called Prem, didn't you? You called him to the temple. You said it was something really important. And he came.'

~

His horror at the thick blood in the temple, the stink, the mess. He had never seen anything like it in his disinfected life. Her clinging arms around his neck, her lips at his ears whispering desperately. 'Take me away! Take me away now. It is our only chance! Please!'

And the boy pulling free, backing away, saying 'No. No. I can't. I've been thinking and maybe—maybe it's not the time for us to get married. We're too young...'

Oh the hurt, the desperation—and then the anger. The anger. The anger of Kali flooding her. Black and awful. Her eyes open wide and she suddenly sees him for what he is. A young pampered boy. So soft that he cowers back from the first test that life throws at him. Denies in one breath all the promises that he had made. The coward!

Anger reaches for a weapon. The boy turns to run and slips in all the blood. He falls and struggles to get to his feet. She stands over him, dark goddess with silver in her upraised hand. He begins to weep. The blade flashes in the darkness.

∼

There was a shocked silence. Then Item rose to her feet with a despairing cry. 'I didn't kill him!' she wailed, 'I didn't!'

Sister's voice was a hand that grabbed her and held her in her place. 'Silence! Not now little one. You will not speak now. All in its time.'

Item collapsed back on the floor her hands held to her mouth to hold back the words that were foaming inside.

Mrs Jindal was an odd mirror image. Her hands too were held to her mouth. She was staring at Item as if she could not absorb the idea of the girl killing her son. 'No,' she said. 'Not her. Not her!'

Sister agreed. 'The little one speaks the truth. She did not kill him. She wasn't strong enough. If she had killed him there would have been no need for another blow. With another weapon. An axe that just a few hours before had been sharpened to hack the head off a goat. As I said—he was killed twice.'

∼

The boy crawling around slipping and sliding in all the blood, trying to hold a hand to his neck. Blood spurting from between his fingers. The strange crowing noises he made. The little one standing there trembling and weeping. Kaali watching it all with her wide eyes.

~

Laalji spoke up in a matter-of-fact voice. 'What did you expect me to do? He was dying already. I put him out of his agony.'

There was a sudden shriek. It was Mrs Jindal. She launched herself at Laalji, her hands curved into claws. Inspector Rakesh managed to get to her in time and found himself struggling with an armful of scented fury.

'You killed him! You killed my son!'

It took the combined effort of Sister and the Inspector to hold her still. She twisted in their grasp and spat at Laalji. All the veneer of sophistication was gone.

'Enough!' said Sister, 'we have not finished. There is one more murder to be explained. Sit.' Mrs Jindal sat, dishevelled and weeping in anger. The Inspector kept a wary eye on her. He had a scratch down the side of his face that stung. Laalji wiped the spit off his face and said nothing.

'The evening Sethna died there was a perfume in that room. A scent specially mixed for a rich lady.' Sister turns to Mrs Jindal. 'You came to see him.'

Mrs Jindal spoke in a hoarse agonized whisper. 'I wanted to know who had killed my son. I knew that Sethna would know. But I stopped at the door because I remembered I had perfume on. He would have never let me in. I called from the door. But no one answered, which was strange. I stepped in and he was dead. Lying on that bed, dead.'

She turned to Sister. 'You have to believe me. I never killed him. I found him dead, and I ran from the place.'

'I believe you,' said Sister. 'You did not kill him. He was killed by love.'

Sister turned to Laalji and spoke to him directly. 'Love. It is such a terrible thing. You went to meet Sethna to demand a new price for the murder that had taken place at your hands. A new price for your silence. You wanted Item.'

Laalji gave no evidence that he had heard. His eyes were fixed on Item. She shuddered and drew away from him.

'I think Sethna was right,' said Sister. 'There are only two motives for murder. In this case, both the killings were for love.'

～

The sound of the girl's anklets every Monday in the temple. So demure in front of Kali, but every step a provocation. Bending to light a lamp. Her face a warm glow lit in the darkness. Laughing and brushing past him as she left. Raising her eyes to look directly into his when he gave her prasad. He knew flirting was a habit with her. She did it with all the men. It meant nothing. And still...

～

Item got to her feet. 'It was him!' she said. 'Him. I was angry, but I didn't hurt Prem badly. It was Laalji. He took his axe and he—' She was trembling from head to toe. 'Sethna told me to be quiet. That he would handle it all. To pretend I knew nothing about the murder.' Her voice was scared and young, and she sounded for the first time like the sixteen-year-old she was. 'I was so scared they would find it was me. So I kept saying it was her.' She indicated Mrs Jindal with a trembling finger.

'It's all right, child,' said Sister. 'We know. You can go now. You're free.'

'Free?' said Item, bitterly. 'To do what? Where will I go? Who will look after me? Who do I have?'

The big man sat there, unmoving and expressionless. Laalji never took his eyes from Item. He watched her with sad eyes even as Inspector Rakesh led in the other policemen. Before they could reach him, he finally closed his eyes and bent his head to lay it at Kali's feet. 'As is your will, Mother,' he said.

He went unresisting, turning his head and opening his eyes wide so that he could drink in his last sight of the girl he loved.

~

The Chief got to his feet. 'Well, that wraps up the case. Thank you, Inspector. Thank you, Sister, for your help.' The temple began to empty.

'The rest of you are free to go,' said Inspector Rakesh. 'Except you, Mrs Jindal, we'd like a word with you.'

Mrs Jindal had taken tissues from her bag. She was trying to wipe her ravaged face and reassemble herself, but her hands were trembling too much. 'What could you possibly want with me, now?' she said. Slow tears kept running down her face.

'Please wait,' said Sister. 'I wish to have a private word with you.'

'I would not recommend it at all,' said the lawyer. 'We are done here. Let us leave.'

'Please,' said Sister.

Mrs Jindal sent her lawyer to sit in the car, ignoring his protests.

∼

They spoke with only Kali to hear them.

'I know,' said Sister simply.

Mrs Jindal looked up at her. 'Another photograph that Sethna couldn't resist keeping?' she asked bitterly.

Sister shook her head. 'When you spat at Laalji—the resemblance was unmistakable.'

Inspector Rakesh spoke up. 'And I assembled all the accounts that Sethna kept. You had been paying him for nineteen years.'

'She's two years older than Prem. She looks so young. I had her when I was fifteen. I was still breastfeeding her when Jindal came along. Sethna tried to make me give her up for adoption, but I wouldn't.'

∼

*Dancing at night. Breasts sore and weeping. Feeding
the baby hurriedly between songs. Padding the blouses
so that it wouldn't show when her breasts wept. Then
the unexpected suitor. Medicines to make the milk
stop. The child wailing all night long. All the mess
and worry of a fake nath. And in the end it was all
worth it. He wanted to marry her.*

~

'It was my one chance. So, I took it. But I could not
take her with me. I was supposed to be a virgin. I left
her with Sethna. I had some confused idea I would take
her away later. Hide her somewhere. I was so young.'

She looked old now. Old and tired and very sad.
'Her name is Priya. I chose it because I loved her very
much. You always love the first child out of you in a
way that you will love no other.'

'And the payments you made to him?'

'They weren't blackmail. I paid him to look after
her. To make sure that she was okay. I wanted him to
send her to school. Educate her. I wanted to do my
best for her.' She shook her head. 'But she wouldn't
have any of it. She was trouble from the beginning.
Bunking school. Running away. Headstrong.'

'He put her to work dancing.'

Mrs Jindal shook her head. 'That was her. She
wanted to do it. She wanted admiration and pretty
things. She fought with him. Didn't eat for five days.
He phoned me and I came and met him. "She has your
stubbornness," he said, "I can't change her mind."'

She shrugged. 'What could I do? In the end we let her dance. Sethna said he would guard her and make sure he found someone decent for her to marry. This was her life. It was too late to take her away. And then—'

She couldn't say it. Sister said it for her. 'And then the unthinkable happened. Brother fell in love with sister.'

Sister didn't believe in chance. But here it was, undeniable. A boy walks into a bar and falls in love with the one girl in the world that he shouldn't.

'We had to stop it. Sethna and I were desperate. That's when he thought of Laalji. He was supposed to terrify her. That is all.'

She felt silent, regretting all that had unravelled here in the temple from that one decision. 'Now Sethna is gone. What will happen to her I don't know. She won't listen to anyone. She is so wild.' She waved a weary hand. 'I don't care about being Mrs Jindal any more. I have enough money saved. I would take her. But she hates me. How will I ever explain?'

She sat there rocking back and forth, wracked by the torment of a mother who cannot see a way to save the only child left to her.

'I will take her,' said Sister with quiet decision. 'In time, I will make her understand.'

'Why would you do that?'

'Because random kindness is sometimes necessary.'

～

A frightened child crouched by the wall of a temple, bleeding and in too much pain to hear the snicker and click of wooden sticks hitting against each other inside. Fleeing a terror in which he was held down by strong hands, and a blade glinted in the dark. Knowing that he had nowhere to go and he could never go home.

A man standing at the door of the temple and looking down at the child's inadequate hiding place. The child not caring any more. Wanting to die because the pain in his heart was more than the pain between his legs. The man squatting and saying gently, 'You are hurt child. Come. I will heal you.'

~

'Yes,' said Sister, looking back down many years to that beginning. 'Random kindness is all that stands between us and despair.'

SERIAL KILLER

Manjula Padmanabhan

When you're a child, you assume that everyone you know is exactly the same as you. If, for instance, you swallow a mosquito immediately after it's bitten someone else and you realize the taste in your mouth is another person's blood, you assume that everyone would enjoy that moment as much as you do. It doesn't occur to you that you might be wrong. When you do, it's a big shock. You feel outraged and rejected.

Little by little though, you begin to see that each person occupies his or her own individual universe of amusements. You understand that maybe your sister really doesn't like curds or that your brother really does excel at maths. You begin to separate the world into those who have similar interests and those who do not. You accept that these differences are nothing to be concerned about.

When I was growing up, I believed I was completely ordinary and therefore, normal. Being a boy may have had something to do with it: I certainly believed that boys were the definition of normal while girls were a variation. As a grown man I continue to epitomize the unremarkable norm. My hair is black and thick. I am considered medium-tall and I have never been fat. I am clean-shaven and I dress in a similarly clean-cut, unfussy manner.

My father worked in the Railways. We were posted from place to place. We lived in government flats with lime-washed walls and heavy wooden furniture that had file numbers painted onto the sides. Everyone I knew was just like us. I believed this without the slightest question. If someone had tried to argue that maybe, in the statistical sense, in a country composed mostly of miserably struggling villagers, we were far from ordinary, I would have fiercely rejected that view.

I had a younger brother and a sister who was five years younger than him. We had uncles and aunts. They came to visit us wherever we were posted. My mother always had someone to help out in the kitchen and someone to clean the floors. I went to Catholic schools. I didn't get into fights. There were no riots in the places where we lived.

Once, when I was eight years old, there was a derailment of a goods train within the district of my father's jurisdiction. We were stationed in West Bengal. North of Calcutta. There were no passengers inside the train. But two labourers who had hitched a ride on top of one of the ill-fated wagons had lost their lives. The accident happened in the afternoon while my father was home, at lunch. I was still at school.

When the driver came to pick me up from school, Father was in the car. I went along with him to the accident site.

One of the two victims had split open, as if he'd fallen onto a jagged spike on his way down. He'd been ripped open down the middle, like a jute sack. He looked like a peapod except he wasn't green on the inside. Father was too busy to notice that I was there with him. He forgot to tell me to look away.

So I didn't.

Until that moment I had not realized that human beings were similar to all other creatures, on the inside. I'd seen cooks gutting the chickens we ate at home. I had seen goats being slaughtered in the bazaars, at festival times. I had seen their organs spill out. There was a chart in one of my schoolrooms, showing the Human Body, but it was not realistic. It was more like a diagram, showing machine parts. Intellectually, I knew that we contained organs similar to what I'd seen pouring out of other animals but somehow, I had never put it all together. I had not realized that if someone were to cut us up, we'd see those same glistening, jewel-box colours—ivory yellow, turquoise green, lipstick-pink, Coca-Cola brown—within ourselves.

It was on this same occasion of the derailment that I recognized the specific type of rage that filled my chest like a black balloon when faced with a situation in which I couldn't do as I wished. For instance, with that unknown labourer stretched out on the ground,

I was so thrilled and fascinated. That broken exposed body looked to me like a sack of hidden treasures. I wanted to run over to see and to taste and to smell whatever I could.

But of course there was no question of such behaviour. Without even asking, I knew that if I'd mentioned my desire to my father, he would have slapped me across the mouth right there in front of everyone. When we got home, he'd have told my mother and I would've been slapped again.

The knowledge that I was unconcerned about taking lives came shortly after my twelfth birthday. Our cook in Gangtok was called Bahadur. He told me privately that his real name was something quite different, but that it didn't matter; he didn't mind being called Bahadur. One day he brought home two fine white roosters from the market. I was in the backyard when he returned, holding the two birds upside down, by their ankles. They were alert and watchful, their big red heads jerking this way and that, their eyes glittering like orange marbles. They made no sound, however. Nor did they struggle.

When Bahadur saw that I was interested, he called me towards him. I didn't know that he was about to kill the birds. I went to him because he called me. What happened next happened very fast. First he handed me one bird to hold. He gave me no opportunity to back out. He just separated one bird from the other—their legs were tied with a twist of string—and handed it to me. It might have been a pumpkin or a banana stem. I took it from him without a word, surprised again that there was no resistance from the creature.

Then he reached for his big shiny knife that was hanging from a hook just outside the kitchen door and with a single sharp *whack*, severed the head from the body. It was so impressive! My mouth dropped open without my realizing it. For weeks afterwards, Bahadur teased me about it, about my expression.

In the next moment, he handed me the knife. To this day, I can remember the calm blankness that came over me. It was as if we had rehearsed these movements a thousand times. He handed me the knife, politely turning the handle towards me, while the carcass of the bird in his left hand flapped and juddered, cherry-bright blood pouring to the ground from the raw-edged tube that was the dead bird's gullet. I took the knife, raised the second bird up just as Bahadur had done and—*whack!*—severed the head from the body. In one clean swipe.

Bahadur cackled out loud, but when I glanced up at him, the dead chicken's body flapping in my hand, I saw that the expression in his black eyes, contained within the triangular shape made by the creases of his eyelids, was respectful. He was impressed with me and I felt delighted. Later, when his hands were clean, he patted me on the head and praised me for being fearless. For several weeks after that, he called me whenever he brought chickens in from the market and I killed them for him.

Until one day, my mother found out.

She was upstairs in her bedroom and happened to look down. She screamed and called out but was too late to stop me. She ran down nevertheless, into the backyard and dragged me away by my ear. I was still holding the bloodied knife, squealing with pain.

'Drop it,' she said, 'drop the knife, DROP IT!' And at that moment, as I was squirming and wriggling, crying, trying to break free of her grip, an image appeared in my head of me twisting free, becoming a giant, grabbing my mother's neck and—*whack!*— severing her head from her body.

I remember how easily that thought slid into my mind. I remember my unconcern. That is, I placed no greater importance upon the thought of severing my mother's head from her neck than I did the chicken's. I didn't think it was unusual. It was just the way I was structured.

I believe it was the very ordinariness of my life that prevented me from questioning my casual attitude towards death. In the same way that everything about me was commonplace and also normal, so was this ability. Some people can whistle tunes or fix broken clocks. I could dismantle living things. I thought of it as a handy gift. Something that might be useful in later years, say, if I joined the military, or became a secret agent or a superhero. Boys are wont to have these amusing fantasies and I assumed that most other boys around me were no different. If they didn't express these views it was only part of the hidden universe that I assumed everyone had within them.

It would be a while before I understood that my special ability, my 'gift', was regarded with revulsion and fear by society at large. Initially I was puzzled by this realization but not unduly dismayed. We are all different, after all. We each have our private inner worlds.

There are two parts to the gift. The first part is that I feel no reverence towards the body or to what others speak of in hushed tones as 'the miracle of life'. I think of the body as a marvellous machine with soft, pliable parts. Just as I regard a car or a sewing machine as something marvellous but not mystical, I think of bodies, human as well as animal, as exquisitely designed machines. Bodies are destined to breathe, to move, to procreate and ultimately, to die. And that is all. There's no hereafter, no thereafter. No gods, no angels, no devils or monsters. No mystery.

The second part is, I do not feel anything in the way of morality. It's the same as being blind or deaf except there's no organ of morality, such as an eye or an ear. Just as a deaf or blind person has to adjust himself to the norms of the general population, I too have had to live my thirty-odd years pretending that I can distinguish between right and wrong the same as anyone else. Unlike a physically challenged person, however, I cannot reveal my disability. To lack a moral compass is to be regarded as monstrous after all. Those who believe in morality would consider it their duty to hunt me down and destroy me in the name of all humanity.

The name that might be given to me is 'sociopath'. The fact that I would be reviled and hated by everyone around me, if my condition could be known, does not bother me. It's all a question of relativity. Relative to the general population, sociopaths are rare. Therefore we are despised.

Contrary to popular belief, it's not at all true that sociopaths are cold, unfeeling machines. Speaking for myself, I can say that it's quite the opposite. Lacking a moral compass, I can observe the play of light and shade in everything around me, not just the pretty or the socially acceptable things. I can look at, say, the site of a bomb blast or a natural disaster with aesthetic detachment so that I see it as an abstract composition of splintered limbs and bloated bodies. My ears can receive the shriek of a dog being hit by a car in the street as a distinct flavour—anguish, despair, terror—and savour it right alongside the shrieks of a violin being played in an orchestra.

I think of myself as different. That's all. Certainly not sinful, because I don't believe there is such a thing as sin. It's a part of my private life, something that I've managed to conceal for a long time. There are those who conceal their sexual interest in little children. I conceal my interest in taking lives. Ever since my first victim, at age seventeen, I have lived this double life. There are times when I have yearned to lean forward during some moronic debate about right and wrong, to say, 'Oh come on! It's just death, you know? It's nothing. It's commonplace. It's happening right now, all over the world, in all kinds of ways. Get over it.'

My first human victim was someone I encountered on board a night train. A small, sooty thief. I was seventeen and we were living in Delhi those days. I was in a first class reserved compartment which I had all to myself, on my way to Bikaner. I had what old-timers like my father called a 'coupé'—a narrow compartment with just two bunks. If you made the booking through a 'contact' then you could get one of these to yourself. For me and for anyone connected to my father, making bookings through a 'contact' was the only way we knew how to travel.

It was common knowledge that trains leaving the Old Delhi railway station were preyed upon by 'robbers', or 'dacoits' or those going by some other similar name. It was the kind of incident that regular commuters accepted with a shrug, saying 'these things happen!' after which they would swap stories of horror and tragedy that they had heard of, though never actually experienced. Passengers were cautioned against opening the doors of their compartments to strangers, particularly if the train happened to halt unexpectedly between stations at night.

I wasn't even slightly concerned. Living as I did in the protected bubble of the Railways' services, where I was used to getting special treatment, I rarely had to think twice about security or personal safety. At night, I locked the door to my compartment the way I always did, because otherwise the door would swing open and shut, with an irritating clacking sound. It was ordinary first class, not A/c and I had left the window open. Like I said, no concern for safety even crossed my mind. I turned the light off and fell asleep quickly.

At some time in the night, a child must have attached himself to the outer skin of the train just as we were pulling out of one of the smaller, suburban stations. There are dozens of ways that a small, scrawny body can climb onto a train and remain as unnoticed as an adventurous rat—say from a water tower or the underside of an overbridge. Once on the train, he would have had to creep carefully along, finding toeholds and fingerholds as he moved, matching his movements to the jogging rhythm of the great iron animal he was clinging to.

These are all guesses. What I know is only what happened once the boy wriggled in through the window of my coupé, yes, through the bars, because he was so thin and lithe, only to land with an ungainly crash upon a stack of stainless steel utensils that I had placed against the window-side wall of the compartment.

Perhaps he was weak from hunger and fell into the coupé rather than climbed into it with care. Perhaps the train gave an extra jerk at exactly the wrong moment for him. I won't ever know why he was so clumsy that one fatal time in his short life. Whatever the reason, the result was that I woke up as if a bullet had struck my sleeping brain. In the next instant, with the dazzling clarity brought on by shock, I saw the source of the crash, fell out of bed and grabbed the small figure.

I remember how he felt in my hands: just like one of Bahadur's chickens, except that he was bigger and refused to remain still. He was jittering and jigging about like a crazed thing. From raw instinct, in the dark and on the floor of that rocking, speeding, rattling train, I had grabbed him by the neck and pinned him to the floor. I struggled to my feet—first my knees, then my feet—as he kicked and struggled and even tried to bite my wrist. But it was futile. I stood up, picked him off the ground and shook him. Shook him like a dog shakes a bandicoot in its teeth. Shook him until suddenly he went limp. And was dead.

What a moment that was.

I was panting, trembling from head to foot, rivers of sweat pouring from me. I hadn't uttered a single sound. I was swaying with the motion of the train. I can't be sure if it's my faulty memory or a fact but I seem to recall that at exactly the right moment, the train's engine gave out a long triumphant HOOOOooooooooOOOOOOT! A wild, pagan shriek that might have been ripped from my own throat. HOOOOooooooooOOOOOOT! I felt wonderful.

My whole body was engulfed in rapture of a kind that I had never dreamed might be available to me. At that time I had not yet had sex with a woman, nor taken drugs nor ever gotten severely drunk. I thought I was ordinary, remember? I believed I had a minor gift, but I didn't think there was anything remarkable about it. I had no idea, until that moment, that the gift provided such a powerful kick.

The train was still moving at full click. I realized that getting rid of the body was an immediate priority. I didn't waste any time thinking through my actions—I knew there was only one thing to be done and that was to bundle the small body out, the same way it had entered: through the window. We were flying across the lightless wastelands to the south and west of the city. The child's body would lie where it fell until wild animals and vultures found it. It would be consumed, digested and forgotten. The child would vanish as completely as if he had never existed in the first place.

～

Absurd as it may sound, I look upon that first kill in the same light as the moment of revelation described by those who claim to have found God. I no longer had doubts. Instead I had a path. I had found myself. I had become an addict who had been exposed for the first time to the drug that would control his life from then on.

Until that moment, my choice of career had been unclear to me. My parents would have dearly wanted me to follow in my father's footsteps. Failing that, the police. Or the armed services. I have uncles in the air force. One in the navy.

After the train incident, however, I knew that no form of government service would be suitable. The constant scrutiny, the peons and ADCs, the settled, respectable life—no, no, it was all completely out of the question. My parents were not especially rich, but they could afford to send me to medical school. I tried it for a couple of years before deciding that the far better path, the one that suited me on so many levels at once, was veterinary medicine.

It may come as a surprise, but I adore animals. I love their uncomplicated, furry-faced enthusiasms: food, sex and a safe place to sleep. What more is there to life? They in turn love me. Running a clinic meant that I had the ideal tools for pursuing my clandestine interests.

My parents retired to Chennai. A mere seven years after the Train Incident I had opened a clinic close to our family home, on a tree-lined avenue in Chetpet. My clients lived all around me, in cement-roofed properties with high walls surrounding well-tended gardens. I'm no socialist but I feel an instinctive contempt for the idle rich. People who live in their silk-lined cocoons of wealth, sustained by the sweat of their domestic help and the countless millions of less-privileged toilers who grow their food and manufacture their possessions. By contrast, whatever I own, whatever I or my parents have achieved, it has all been hard won through work and ability.

The fact that the majority of my clients came from these privileged homes didn't bother me. I feel an instinctive sympathy for animals. It was the impressionable young women who were their typical owners, who had a negative effect on me. I considered their naïvete a type of arrogance: I saw it as a symptom of their absolute blindness to the social injustices that stained the world around themselves.

I enjoyed imagining the horrified expressions that would appear on their faces if they could but know of my secret life! Fortunately for them and for myself, I had no interest in interrupting the flow of their tediously frilly lives. I had found a niche for myself and was very content.

While my younger siblings had spread their wings and fulfilled the ambitions of their generation, I had stayed at home with my parents. They lived in the way of successful middle class people enjoying their retirement. They had a single-storey house, a garden, two cars and a driver. As their eldest son, I enjoyed the status of Highly Eligible Bachelor On The Block, without feeling the need to tie myself down just yet. I know, from the fawning behaviour of the girls who come to my clinic, that I am considered reasonably good-looking.

My clinic soon became very popular. As soon as I could afford it, I bought a larger property in one of the nearby avenues and expanded the facilities to include a short-stay kennel for dogs. I had a junior vet who handled emergencies and the morning schedule, plus three permanent staff members and four daily-wagers who came and went on a rotating schedule.

I had two big dogs of my own, two Doberman Pinschers called Timmy and Tilly. They absorbed the full force of my emotional needs. The combination of clinic and kennel afforded me a very good living though I preferred to keep this fact hidden from sight. Being conspicuously wealthy in a country seething with desperately poor people was the same as wearing a deer-costume in the forest during the hunting season.

Once every four or five months, I satisfied the demands of my secret life. I identified a victim and began a process of vetting to confirm whether or not he was suitable. I was meticulous. I was tidy. Very much the bureaucrat. I even kept records, complete with code words to cover my tracks. A typical campaign lasted three to six months. I didn't mind prolonging the preparations with fussy attention to detail. So far I had not failed once, nor caused so much as a single line of enquiry to appear in the press.

It amused me to know that, despite my occasional girlfriends, there were rumours that I Must Be Gay. Why? Because nowadays that's what Indians think of men who are not married by the age of thirty. There is never the least suspicion that my obsessions might lie in some other direction altogether. Really, I am frequently shaken to realize how wantonly innocent the average person is.

This, then, is the background against which, two months ago, I received a call on my clinic's cell. It was a Sunday and I was at home, relaxing in the TV room. Timmy and Tilly were snoring at my feet. My mother was in the garden, chivvying the gardener to do her bidding. My father was at the dining table, reading the newspaper.

The voice at the other end of the call suggested a young woman but not a girl. 'Doctor?' she said. 'Dr Shankar?' When I confirmed my identity, she said she had an elderly dog that needed urgent assistance. 'I know it's a Sunday. You might not be able to come…' She paused to draw a breath, as if uncertain whether or not to proceed. 'I'm sorry I've not said my name. I'm Jessica. Actually I came to see you the other day. Along with my friend Pressy. With the French Bulldog? Bijou?'

Yes, I remembered. I smiled as I said, 'Ah…yes. I remember Bijou!' This was my subtle warning shot: *it's your friend's dog that made an impression on me. Not the owner. And certainly not you.* Yet this was a lie. I have always been very observant. So I remembered the plump-cheeked girl called Pressy who talked too much. Beside her, behind her, had stood her friend. She'd been introduced as 'Jessa'. I had noticed her because of the way she had made a point of standing apart. As if disengaged from the situation.

Bijou had needed his nails clipped and a general tune up. Pressy prattled on as I attended to the diminutive animal, white with black ears and nose. He was a young dog, and in good condition. Not yet neutered though Pressy wanted to know when would be a good time to bring him in for '…you know, the snip-snip…' Through it all, I was conscious of this other presence, just at the edge of my vision, an oddly solid figure, medium tall, dressed in dark-on-dark jeans and top.

I am very careful where I place my eyes, in the clinic. Young women are so very self-conscious these days. A glance here, an over-friendly smile there and before you know it, the word has gone out that nice Dr Shankar is not so nice after all.

So I didn't look directly at that other presence right behind Pressy until it was time for them to leave. Then I glanced up, my expression entirely bland and professional. In a few seconds I gleaned the rest of the impression: yes, the shoulders were indeed a bit wider than was typical in Indian women. The clothes were quiet in the way of someone who is confident enough not to seek attention. The hands were unadorned: no nail polish, no rings. The feet were in flat-heeled casuals, made for walking rather than socializing.

And the face? Yes, the face was definitely interesting. Hair tied back, a strong nose, eyebrows in a straight line, very carefully plucked to seem unplucked and the extremely smooth skin of the well-tended rich. She looked me full in the face. Her mouth curled up at the corners. It was not an expression, but the shape of the mouth. It had a slight smile built into it. Then she turned her head, even as I nodded my goodbyes and my assistant saw them both out.

All these impressions came back to me as she explained on the phone about her dog. Old, sick, requiring urgent attention.

Ordinarily, it would have been unthinkable for me to entertain her request, to go out to where she lived, far away, in Adyar, on a Sunday. My curiosity was piqued, however. It's hard to explain, but I felt sure she was lying. Perhaps, intuitively, I knew it was too soon after Bijou's visit for an emergency to have risen, so soon, so conveniently, that would require me to drive out to see her. Perhaps it was the audacity of the request. Who calls a vet, requesting a house call, when there's never even been a first-visit before?

Only a supremely confident person. Someone used to being obeyed.

I smiled to myself, as I said to her, 'It's all right. I'll make an exception.' I smiled because it amused me to let Jessica play her game for a few more turns.

Maybe I was also genuinely intrigued and interested. It is rare, after all, for young Indian women to be so coolly assertive. They were capable of being brash, vulgar, silly and embarrassingly direct, but cool? Confident? No. That was unusual. It would be interesting to discover the source of the confidence. To puncture it, perhaps, or to be disappointed. I was open to the gamut of possibilities. I was fancy-free at the moment and could imagine being attracted to her, though she wasn't what I thought of as 'my type'. I am attracted to confident, charismatic women in the abstract, when I see them in films for instance, or read about them in books. In reality I prefer the shallow frivolity of the traditional feminine type.

Half an hour later, I was in the car and on my way. I wore Sunday casuals: a white polo shirt and pale cream slacks. The GPS found the address for me easily enough, one of the fortress-like beach-front properties.

There was a sentry-box at the gate. Once within the grounds, a uniformed valet took my keys from me to park the car. Unpolished granite surfaces were much in evidence, with three huge fan palms serving as screens between the driveway and the house. The first impression I had was of a hotel, not a residential home. It's true of many wealthy homes these days.

Jessica was waiting for me by the curb. I got down from the car, bringing my doctor's kit with me. She was dressed in a black top and loose white shorts that extended down to her knees. Her feet were bare. She wore no jewellery except for a thin gold band around her right ankle. Her hair was tied back in a single thick plait. 'Thank you so much for coming, Doctor,' she said. 'You have no idea how much it means to me.'

She ushered me in to a cool dark interior, across a hall and into another room. The dog was lying in state, on its side, on its own mattress, right by the floor-to-ceiling windows that looked out onto a front lawn. In the distance was a fence and beyond it, though invisible from the house, was the sea.

The dog was immense, a Great Dane. I murmured something soothing as I looked him over, kneeling by his side. He was breathing in slow, deep strokes, fast asleep. He was a beauty. Dark muzzle, ears clipped, tail docked, brindled coat. White socks on his forepaws. Neutered.

He wasn't old. Five years at the outside? And as for unwell, from what I could tell at first glance, he was simply very deeply asleep. In the manner of an animal that has been drugged. So as I knelt beside him, gently feeling behind his ears, his throat, palpating his abdomen, the only question in my mind was, whether to play along with Jessica's deception. I could prescribe a medication and leave. Or I could call her bluff.

I got to my feet and, stalling for time, asking to be shown to a washroom. When I came out, she was standing nearby, in the glass-fronted hall that looked out onto the same vista as the room in which the dog lay. As I approached her, she turned and said, 'Would you like to go out? To the lawn?'

It was as easy as that. No need for lies and explanations. She knew that I knew and she decided to move past that knowledge. I felt a curious tingling along the back of my neck. It is very unusual for me to be in a situation in which I don't know the nature of the path on which I will place my next steps.

As if to lock that uncertainty into place, I left my sandals in the hall and we walked out onto the grass, cool and green despite the nodding shade of different varieties of tall palms. There must be full-time gardeners here, and plenty of water, to maintain such a lawn.

We walked to the fence and looked towards the sea. She asked me to stay for lunch. I said, 'Some other time,' but agreed to have tea. We remained outside, in a shaded alcove at the front of the house. A current of cool air flushed down out of a vent above us, cooling us even as we sat in the mild humidity of a January afternoon. Tea was brought to us by a woman servant in a dark blue sari.

Jessica spoke easily about herself. Her parents lived in Singapore, which was where she had grown up. She had chosen her first name for herself, when she was twelve years old, based on a cartoon character. This house we were in was built with her parents' money, though it housed her paternal grandparents. She'd studied to be a lawyer but when it came to joining a firm, decided to take a break. The question of what she'd been doing during this break remained dangling in the air. I reciprocated by talking about my patients, my fondness for animals, my preference for dogs and my lack of experience with small reptiles such as chameleons.

Then a dimple of silence developed into which we would either pour a second cup of tea or...'Doctor, I think you should know that I have been stalking you for some time.' She had been looking away but now she moved her gaze back to me. Square in the eye.

Here it comes, I thought. 'Is that so?' I said. My voice remained entirely neutral and I gazed back at her as if I had nothing to hide. It is possible, as I have known for a very long time, to lie outright, while staring straight into someone's eyes. Indeed, if one is going to lie, that is the only way to do it.

'Yes,' she said. 'Maybe there is something more for us to talk about. Or maybe not. I really do not know. If there is, you will get back in touch with me.' The smile in her mouth twitched upwards very slightly. 'If there is not, you will not see me again.'

I glanced at her and in that moment, I had the

uncomfortable notion that she could see right through me. Straight through all the layers of carefully maintained pretences, to my untidy secret interior. It was a thing that had never happened to me before. Never ever.

Of course it was a ridiculous notion: she was merely well trained as a lawyer. It was part of her kit of professional tools to give an impression of all-knowing wisdom. So I blinked, smiled and prepared to stand up. 'That would be a shame,' is how I responded, in a light, sociable voice.

'Yes,' she said. Then I took her leave and drove home. My stomach was growling with hunger while my mind was prickling over with violent, radioactive curiosity.

My entire life has been one of extreme, exquisite deliberation. I have no choice: after all, I do not want to be found out. It isn't simply that I make careful plans for every moment of my day, but that I have contingencies for all possible alternative outcomes, reaching far into the future. Well, not *all*, of course, because that would be pointlessly time-consuming. Still. I have trained myself to find my way quickly through the most likely series of possibilities to recognize the paths that might yield the best results. I had been doing this for so long, and with so little conscious effort, that for all practical purposes I am almost never taken by surprise.

Now here I was! Faced with an enigma.

For several days afterwards, I simply created a

bubble around the subject of Jessica and avoided thinking about her. Normally, I have no difficulty circumventing unproductive thoughts or ideas. The problem here was that I wasn't sure whether or not I needed to know what she knew. In order to be sure, I needed to get back in touch with Jessica. Yet I didn't want to do that. I hated feeling manipulated.

Of course I Googled her. Looked her up on Facebook and Twitter. Followed her social media footprint at other sites. Nothing startling. A boyfriend or two, funny hats at funny parties, that sort of thing. Her dog's name was Trivia, I learnt. He was four and a half years old. Puppy pictures. She had a younger brother who lived in Singapore with her parents, studying interior design. He appeared to be gay and had a number of pretty-boy friends.

Once, when I was on Facebook, I noticed that her profile icon was live. She was online. If I sent her a friend request and if she accepted it, we could chat. But I didn't send a request. That would be the same as 'getting in touch with her' and she would know that she had won the toss.

I alternated between feeling extremely irritated with her for putting me through this uncertainty and strangely, perversely attracted. I had moments when I felt, irrationally, that she was watching me from a distance, enjoying my frustration. I had never felt this way before.

Adding to my frustration was the fact that I was at the halfway mark in what I had hoped would be my next campaign. Now I felt I couldn't proceed. Not when I knew that someone was, as she put it, 'stalking' me. Of all the things she had said, this was the most disturbing to me. I am by nature very, very careful. I cover my traces. For instance, I have more than one car for my personal use. Three, actually, with two of them hidden. This was to ensure that I could go out on a sortie without my transport being recognized.

For her to say that she stalked me was just ridiculous. In the first place, she could be lying. She could be the sort of person who throws out provocative remarks in the way that some people throw a grenade into a lake as a way of fishing. The remark might be pure mischief, just to see what might float to the surface if I happened to have something to hide—an illicit affair, say, or some petty crime. It couldn't possibly mean that she had literally been following me around.

Could it?

Some days, I said to myself, *So what if she has stalked me? So what if she knows about the other cars?* It means nothing. Anyone might have more than one car. There might be all kinds of explanations. Even if she knew that I had more than one car, it didn't mean that she knew anything else.

Other days, however, I felt certain that her knowing air was a sign that she really did have more information than I wanted her—or anyone—to have. Which led to further questions: if she had seen something, what had it been? How much had she seen?

And most importantly, why had she done nothing about it? Other than make contact with me, that is.

Then I would stop the squirrel-wheel of my thoughts and distract myself with something else altogether. I found myself playing online chess with multiple partners and visiting dance clubs at night. Needless to say, however much I attempted to distract myself, eventually my mind would cycle around to the topic of Jessica and the questions.

In the end, it took a mere three weeks for my resolve to disintegrate. If I wanted answers to my questions, I had to get back in touch. I even considered stalking *her* before deciding that was pretty much the same as giving up and calling. I began to think that she had known all along that I would call, in which case I was only prolonging my agony by delaying.

So I called her. I was grateful that she did not bother to say 'I told you so!' or anything of the sort. At the same time, I felt sure that she was smiling to herself. Feeling smug. Knowing that she had forced me to crawl. I could feel a charge of anger building up, but there was nothing I could do to shake it off.

We made a date to meet for lunch. Then we went out for dinner a couple of times. Each time, our conversations were utterly bland and empty of meaning. She gave me no opportunities to ask for more information while all the time remaining maddeningly self-possessed, as if she had a hidden agenda that she would choose the time and place to reveal. Then on the fourth occasion when I called her, instead of the usual talk about where we would meet and when, she said, 'Doc...'—that's what she called me, 'Doc'—'...I think you should come home once more. Come in the evening. Spend the night.'

It was characteristic of her to be breathtakingly direct. Nothing in her voice made it sound like a romantic invitation. That was the odd, the amazing thing. Instantly, I guessed that this would be the occasion when I would finally get to understand what was behind her mysterious attitude.

I said, 'I don't think I can spend the night. My dogs miss me if I don't come home.'

'Bring them along,' she said. 'Trivia likes company.'

I laughed uneasily. No, I wouldn't do that. My dogs aren't all that friendly. They would consider it bizarre to be taken out on a night-spend. We batted the subject back and forth lightheartedly for a bit, then she said, 'Whatever. It's up to you. But please. Just come over, all right? I think it's time.'

My heart began to hammer in my chest. I couldn't for the life of me fathom what she meant by 'it's time'! Trying not to stammer like an adolescent boy talking to his first crush, I set up a tentative date. When I switched my phone off, I wondered if this was what other people felt like when they fell in love. I did not like the sensation. I preferred to be in control. At the same time, I couldn't deny that I felt a powerful force drawing me towards the woman. It was not a romantic attraction. More like a form of extreme curiosity, with a flickering edge of anxiety: in case she *did* know something incriminating about me, I'd have no choice but to eliminate her. My skin shrank from such a task.

Aside from that one time in my distant youth when I'd wanted to attack my mother, I'd never felt the slightest urge to harm a woman. I don't know enough about my 'condition'—my gift, as I call it—to say whether or not it was because I liked women or because I felt repugnance.

Given my choice of victims and my reasons for choosing them, the issue of targeting women never arose. I had only ever approached men and my motivation had nothing to do with anger or resentment. I felt a clinical detachment, followed by extraordinary pleasure and release after the act.

My entire approach to being what I am, a serial killer, a sociopath, was one of cool deliberation. I even had a justification worked out, something that satisfied my bourgeois need to feel that I was doing good, despite the obvious badness. I had never targeted anyone of my social status, nor acted out of an emotional impulse. Therefore, to 'eliminate' Jessica would go against every principle I had so far followed, of only choosing victims with whom I had no connection, no history, no relationship.

On the designated day, I told my parents some story about a weekend away with school friends and set off. I took both my dogs with me. Just as Jessa— that is what I now called her—had assured me, Timmy and Tilly were wholly unfazed by their unfamiliar surroundings when we reached her house. Trivia greeted them like a tall, loving uncle even though he was the youngest of the three. In no time at all, they were gambolling across the lawn in that carefree way that happy dogs have, as if they'd known each other all their lives.

By contrast, I was tense and irritable. I had always been able to reason my way out of difficult situations, yet here I was, stuck in a dimensionless tunnel, with only the weakest justification for having got into it to begin with.

I was impatient to get on with the revelation that Jessa had promised on the phone. Instead, she introduced me to her grandparents shortly after I arrived and it became clear that we would eat dinner together, in the formal dining room. The irritation buzzing at the back of my mind grew into a thundercloud within me as Jessa and her grandparents engaged me in boneless, genteel-talk about culture and politics all through the interminable traditional vegetarian meal.

By the time we were done, I was afraid that if I so much as opened my mouth, I would bark or howl. The anger within me had grown into a demonic presence, bulging inside my throat. It had been many years since I had felt anything like this and it shocked me. I preferred to be calm and serene. When Jessa suggested that we might take a walk along the darkened shore of the sea after dinner, I leapt at the invitation even as I worried that I would be unable to prevent myself from hitting her or strangling her, if she said something that set me off.

We made our way out via the front of the lawn, through a gate in the fence and onto the scrubby land that preceded the actual beach. Jessa was wearing a long shift, loose and white, that flapped in the wind. I was wearing denim Bermudas, also loose, and a tee-shirt. We had flip-flops on our feet. 'We don't actually own our portion of the beach,' Jessa was explaining. The fishermen's village, a short distance away, had prior rights. 'But there's an informal understanding that permits us access to the sea directly in front of our property.'

The land rose up slightly, fringed with tall grasses. As soon as we crested the rise and started down the slope, the lighted world of the house behind us snapped off. The darkness was so intense and so unexpected, my breath was knocked out of me. The limitless shoreline. The immense horizon. The speckled black vault of night arcing over us. The languid expanse of sand in front of us. The hushed boom of the ocean.

It was too much for me. Too much.

I felt the seams of my inner self crack open like a deep-sea fish responding to the sudden change of pressure at the surface. I felt myself splitting open. I could literally hear sounds inside my head, of crockery being smashed, of light bulbs exploding. The entire contents of my life spilled out of me, the secrets, the tensions, the anxieties—but all in silence and invisible, experienced only by me.

Meanwhile, Jessa walked a little ahead. The dogs, who had accompanied us outside, galloped away, mad with delight.

My thoughts were in turmoil. I could feel a convulsive shivering within my gut, brought on in part by the sharp clean breeze, in part by the pulse of violence that had been lurking within me all evening and was now right on top of my skin. Even as Jessa and I walked together in apparent friendship, in my mind, I could see myself reaching for the woman beside me and squeezing her neck until her eyes popped from her skull. The images in my mind were limned with flame and the energy in my hands and shoulders was like lava coursing in and out of my veins. I could feel my lips aching to draw back in a rabid snarl. I was panting.

Yet all of it remained in my head. I didn't physically do anything or say anything.

The tide was out, so we could walk straight forward a fair distance along that portion of the sand from which the water had withdrawn, leaving it damp and firm. Underfoot, the silky grain of the sand was interrupted with bumps, knobbles and occasional sharp shards of shell. I returned gradually to my senses, calming down in slow stages, until by the time we were at the water's edge, I was normal again. I bent down to touch one gently lapping wavelet after another, each with its delicate ruff of foam. Washed my hands and straightened up again. Turned to look at Jessa.

Finally I could bring the words out into the open, words that had been dammed up inside me for several weeks now: 'What exactly do you know, Jessa?'

She was not looking in my direction and anyway, it was too dark to read her expression. From the sound of her voice, however, I knew she was smiling. 'I can't be sure. I've only seen a part of it. Like I told you right at the beginning? I have stalked you. Followed you on your nocturnal outings. I know where you go, some of the places anyway. I know how you find your, I'm guessing this, your...'—she paused before she said the word—'...victims.'

It was surreal. I had never expected to hear such words from anyone. It was hard for me to accept this was happening at all.

'It's not been all that difficult. Once I knew what to expect, I knew how to anticipate your movements. I learnt about the second car by pure chance. I happened to notice you one night, as your car passed under a street lamp and I recognized you. Then when I had followed you a couple of times, keeping a safe distance from you and I knew the general direction in which you were going. It was enough to remain parked and to await your return. You're a person of habit and you prefer to use familiar routes. Maybe you've grown accustomed to getting away with it. Being invisible. And besides, at night there's hardly any traffic. Keeping track of you was easy.'

I waited for a couple of pulse beats. 'That's all you did? Followed my movements?' I had never expected to have a conversation like this. Never planned to. Never wanted to. There were so many questions, so many thoughts, crowding at the front of my brain. Why me? In what way had I slipped up? How much did she know? And also: Now what? Now what? Now what?

'The rest...well, it's all conjecture, you know.'

All this while, the dogs had been racing about, having their fun. My dogs, who had never encountered the sea before, were alternately afraid and enthralled. All three animals were some distance from us, when Jessa raised her hand to her mouth and did something which I realized a moment later was to blow into a dog-whistle. I heard nothing, but instantly, Trivia stopped in his tracks, wheeled around and began trotting back towards us. Timmy and Tilly followed suit, but more slowly. They were not used to responding to the ultrasonic whistle. They must have heard the sound, saw what their new best friend was doing and followed suit.

I hadn't reacted to Jessa's last remark. She continued now. 'It was the dogs, you know. They were what caught my attention. Tweaked my interest.'

When I said I didn't understand, she turned her head towards me and said, her voice loaded with something similar to laughter, 'Oh yes, you do! You understand very well.'

We turned then and we walked back up the beach in silence. Eventually we sat down on the dry sand, just as it rose up to the crest behind us. I hadn't noticed that she'd brought a cloth bag with her and in it, a light mat to spread on the sand. She told me that she'd bought Trivia from a breeder who had spoken highly of my clinic. But it didn't make sense for her to come all the way to Chetpet from Adyar.

Then her friend Pressy mentioned me too. The Pet Vet of Chetpet. That I had two big dogs. That I was swoon-worthy and a great catch. Except for the rumour that I was gay. Then she met me, that time when she accompanied Pressy with Bijou. That sealed it for her, she said.

'It was something in the way you behaved. It caught my attention. Believe me, you didn't make any wrong moves or say anything out of line. It wasn't just that you were cute either—oh, of course you are—but that wasn't it. There was something else. Something hidden. You were a man who had a secret life and yet you'd grown so comfortable with it, you were so confident about hiding in plain sight, that you didn't have to actually do anything to conceal yourself. You weren't gay, I felt sure of that. Gay men have a different vibe. They're defensive or they're out there or they're repressed. Whichever way they are, however, it's only within the familiar spectrum of sex. Everyone understands sex. It's an itch that everyone has to scratch at some time or another and if some people need to hide the particular places in which they scratch, well, that's just—' she shrugged. 'Just how it is.'

All the while, as she talked, though I was calm, my

mind was scrolling through my options. They weren't good ones. Yet there had to be options. *There had to be.* I realized that she wouldn't have gone to all this trouble unless she had some further point to make. She hadn't come to it yet, but once she did, I'd have to make a decision. I had to be prepared for it. The next logical step for her, I thought, had to be blackmail. Yet it didn't make sense. She couldn't be interested in money, because she already had that. Surely it wasn't something as mundane as romance or marriage! So what could it be? Once more, she had the advantage.

She had fallen silent, I realized, without my recalling what her final words had been. She had used the dog-whistle once more and Trivia came loping up with the other two in tow. For a few moments we were fending off the spray of sand from the dogs' churning paws.

Then, with Trivia lying down beside her, his huge head in her lap, Jessa said, 'Everything was, of course, much harder for me. Every part of it.'

She turned her head and looked me full in the face in that over-direct way she had. It was only then, with blinding clarity, that I understood. I understood what was behind her X-ray vision. What there was about her that seemed so utterly different to anyone else I had ever met. Why she had seen in me what no one else had seen so far.

Because she was the same as me.

'My first one was a nineteen-year-old boy,' she said. A servant in the house. On this property but when it was still a traditional three-storey building with deep verandahs and peaked roofs. It was a common tale, with an uncommon ending.

'He was always a nuisance and he could never keep his eyes to himself. Maybe he had a drinking problem too, I don't know. There was an old cook who had been with the family for ages and this guy was just the young bearer type who stays for three months before being chucked out for one reason or another. He didn't exist for me, I didn't pay any attention to him. But one night, he entered my bedroom just after I had returned from a party. I was in the bathroom when he entered and when I came out, there he was. Completely plastered. He was grabbing his crotch with one hand and in the other hand, he had a knife.'

She smiled.

'I was high too, I suppose, from the party. The main thing, though, was that I wasn't scared. Not at all. I had my skimpy little nightie on and the lights in the room were dim, but I could see perfectly clearly. As he staggered towards me, my mind was diamond-sharp. It was as if I could see into the future, in high-definition slow motion. I saw myself sidestepping as he lunged forward, I saw myself slipping the knife out of his sweaty hand and thrusting it into his throat as he went past me. It was a big knife, and very sharp and everything happened exactly as it appeared in my head.

'A moment later, he was on floor and writhing horribly, gurgling, blood gushing in every direction. He took several minutes to die, after which he was still.

'My room was on the third floor. My grandparents were on the ground floor. It was two or three a.m. There was no one to hear or to see anything. I felt nothing. No guilt, no shame, no fear or disgust. Just a sizzling energy, as if my mind and body had been plugged into the mains. Looking down at the pool of bright blood. Then feeling a trickle on my face, and a liquid enter my mouth and I tasted that same brightness. Blood. And being surprised that it had a taste. Salty, with a touch of iron. Being surprised that I wasn't disgusted or frightened. Quite the opposite.' That's what caught her attention. Instead of horror and anguish at having killed a man, she felt…triumph.

She stopped and glanced at me. 'Yes,' I said. I know what that feels like.

She could easily have told the authorities. She could have easily shown that she had killed him in self-defence. 'But I didn't want to be exposed. The incident would have become a neon-sign hanging over my head. I would be known forever as the Girl Who Killed The Servant Boy and it wouldn't matter where I went or what I did. For the rest of my life, that and that alone would define me.'

Instead she took the second path, the one that so few others would dream of taking. The one that I understood perfectly well: she disposed of the body piece by piece. And told no one.

'Because of the neck wound, he bled like a burst drain. Really gushed. I used four bath towels to sop up most of it, just in case it leaked through the floor tiles or something. The knife he'd brought with him was very sharp, thank goodness. I figured that disposing of the head would be the single most unpleasant task, so my very first move was to cover his face. Instantly, he stopped being a person and became instead a problem to be solved.

'I wrapped the head securely and hacked it away from the body. From biology class I knew that the brain takes in a disproportionate share of the blood in circulation. So I hung the thing over a bucket to drain before going back to deal with the rest of the body.

'It was a Saturday night. I had till Monday morning before the sweeper came in to do my room. Being an old house, the bathroom had one of those huge cast-iron tubs. It was a struggle to get the body into it but you know what? He weighed maybe sixty kilos, not including the head and blood, most of which had drained out. That's about the same as two suitcases. I wrapped the body in a couple of old dressing gowns, tied it up tight, stood inside the tub and then just hauled it in. Like a pair of heavy suitcases, except they were attached to one another. First the legs, then the torso and arms. Into the tub.'

She filled the tub with water, 'because I remember doing dissections, always in a shallow tray filled with water. I cut the body open just like a frog, starting at the pubes and straight up to the throat. Then four sideways cuts, then peeled back the skin. Sure enough, there were the organs all neatly displayed. It was fascinating. Using the same knife, I got the soft organs out and put them in another bucket. From the kitchen, I brought in the liquidizer and ground everything up in it. Heart, lungs, liver, stomach, intestines—it's all just soft meat, after all—I chopped them into small pieces and ground them all up like a puree and flushed the results down the toilet.

'It was around five a.m. by the time I was done. I swabbed the floor with water and slept soundly. I knew I had the whole of Sunday in which to plan what to do with the rest of the body. The feet, hands and the head would pose the greatest challenge because they would be the most recognizable parts of the body. But I knew there was no urgency. I could take my time.'

The next morning, she went to a nearby hardware store and bought a mallet, to physically break down the bones. She pulverized the extremities and smashed the skull, still wrapped tight so that she could empty its contents without being reminded of recognizable features. She liquidized what she could and burned the material she had used to wrap the head in. Then she washed and dried all the teeth and bone fragments carefully and kept them aside inside a small safe in her room.

She had an open terrace, on which she maintained a rooftop garden of palms and frangipani trees. Realizing that it would take her a while to break down the rest of the body, on that Sunday all she did was hack limbs and trunk into manageable portions. She wrapped them tight in plastic garbage bags that she had bought on her trip to the market, to slow down decomposition, then buried them in the earth of her potted plants. Over the course of a week, she removed the flesh, liquidized and flushed it away before smells could develop. The bones meanwhile, were fed to the dogs of her neighbourhood and any other places that she visited.

She took a little extra care over the contents of the safe. She bought a rice-grinder of the kind used to make idli-dosa batter and, installing it in her room, ground down the bone fragments and teeth until they were the texture of coarse sand. She added broken seashells to the mix. Then, while walking along the shore, she scattered the remains of the servant in the surf.

All through the entire experience the one huge lesson she learnt was the same one I had learnt all those many years ago on the train: the reason that time was on her side, the reason we had nothing to fear from our actions was that no one, at any time, would come looking for a corpse.

The boy was unmarried and belonged to what I call the Anonymous Classes. He had a name, but no ID card, no birth certificate. And this was India: the fact that he had vanished from the house without so much as taking his belongings with him would be treated with a shrug and a sigh. His family might write frantic letters and some of his drinking buddies in the locality might come around asking for him but: *there was no body*. Without a body, the police would not be called in. It would not be worth the bother for them.

Within a week, the boy's position had been taken by someone new. Within a month, his memory had begun to fade. Within a year it was as if he had never existed at all.

We lapsed into silence. Jessa's hand stroked Trivia's head absent-mindedly. My own two dogs were arranged near me. She had said the boy had been her 'first', which meant there were other stories to tell. No doubt, in time, I would hear them all.

As she would hear mine. She was correct to surmise that I didn't have to struggle the way she had done. My sorties are planned in advance. I choose derelicts and tramps. I look for those who seem beyond the reach of friendship or family. Old men, exclusively. I look for people who are dishevelled and unkempt in that way that suggests they have long since forgotten what the opposite of such words mean. I look for those who didn't appear to have connections on the street, tracking a potential target for days or for weeks, just to be sure.

It was quite difficult. Street people look out for one another. It's the rare individual who is completely alone, who really has no one. Yet there are a few and eventually I would find them. Sometimes I might chase after them from one location to the next, always taking care to keep my presence and focus of interest discrete. I would leave my car and move around by foot, being sure to dress appropriately. I am patient. I wait until I am certain that it's safe to make my final move, before I bring them into my car.

Sometimes they come in of their own accord. They are used to being shunted around. The police are always doing that. Or social workers. Or other street people. My victims have gone beyond caring what is asked of them. If they are too infirm to move, I help them. The fact that they smell or are covered in sores, body lice and dried shit is of very little concern to me. I am a vet after all. It's all the same to me.

The moment they're in the car, I give them a drink to sedate them. Then I bring them to my clinic, to the back entrance, where I can drive the car into my garage. From there, I have a ramp that leads straight into my basement. It's where I routinely perform surgeries on my animals. There are facilities for various types of procedures including, of course, euthanasia.

I bundle the now inert tramp onto a trolley and roll him down into the basement. I take him to the same area where we bathe and wash our dogs. I clean him up as best I can, aiming to get it done before he's fully awake. I give him a fresh tee-shirt and pajamas. If he is reasonably conscious by then I give him something to eat. It might be a banana or an idli. Maybe a small cup of sambar. These men have forgotten what it is to have an appetite. Their ability to eat is limited.

It is between their final meal and my suggestion that they should take a rest that I give them another dose of sedative. A fatal dose this time. They do not struggle. It's possible they think they're being given medication. I don't know. There's very little conversation.

Yes, it's what we humans call murder. I am taking

a life when I administer my fatal dose. It's not my fault that we live in a world that chooses to devalue entire classes of lives while elevating others to such an extent that I can follow my inclination with no repercussions! Having separated the body from its breath, I process the remains quickly and thoroughly, with all the tools I have at my disposal. Soon, what was once a tramp is a now a collection of plastic-wrapped packages of dog-food. My dogs as well as the residents of the short-stay kennel become the beneficiaries.

I read the same detective fictions and watch the same movies as everyone else. I enjoy the puzzles of logic and forensic investigation that end with the forces of the law triumphant and the deviants safely locked up or killed. But as a deviant myself, I chuckle at all those who think that, with each story, they're celebrating a return to order within the fictional universe of the characters.

Because, of course, I know first-hand that the notion of 'order' is just another fairytale. I have been getting away with my murders for thirteen years now. Each one might be called a mystery, except that no one cares enough to solve it. And that leaves the door wide open for someone like me—a deviant, a monster, a sociopath—to move in on these unfortunate beings who end up on the streets, unwanted and unloved. I give them a sweet death. Then recycle them.

I return from my reverie, as Jessa exclaims softly. I ask her what the matter is.

She says, 'I think I just swallowed a mosquito!'

I smile in the darkness, saying nothing.

BELOVED OF FLOWERS

Uddipana Goswami

As Dino turned to close the rickety iron gate behind him, he felt a drop of something cold fall on the back of his hand. He shuddered. He looked up and realized it was a dewdrop. He felt a strong urge to reach out and touch the tiny drops that he now saw dripping from the translucent petals of the purple flowers overhead. The flowers seemed alive, articulate, about to break into a tale of tormented love, or hate, or perhaps of how love and hate are so often so intertwined in our lives.

Dino felt a shooting pain in his heart at that bittersweet thought. He made a mental note to use it in the next story he wrote. These last few days, it was as if he had been living from one story to the next. He had wanted to continue writing without a break and not be distracted but then he had been summoned to the big house. He had walked over the hill and down again grudgingly, clinging to the broad strap of the cloth bag hanging from his shoulder. His pen and white ream of paper were tucked away in the bag.

But here was a new story the flowers were telling him now, if only he could hear it and record it. They were blooming breathlessly on the bare body of the nearly leafless climber that had twisted itself around the iron archway stretching from one concrete pillar to the other on either side of the gate. Dino could not move. He stood there, looking up.

'Let it be, *kongoxai*! The gate seems to have grown a mind of its own,' Kuxumpriya Baruani baideo's command reached him from the verandah of the house across the driveway.

Dino's trance was broken. With one mighty effort, he managed to align the two halves of the gate and fix the L-shaped latch in the middle. He couldn't just leave it open: that would be most unseemly.

He folded his hands in greeting as he walked down the short driveway to approach the matriarch of the famous Barua clan of Guwahati. In the early days, after the British left, the family owned nearly half of the land in Guwahati, and then some outside the lazily growing city. Till this day, it lived off the land—cultivating some, selling some. And there was more left to spare.

'Who's going to feed off all that land once the old lady's dead?' Tarinikanta often complained. He was Dino's neighbour and now, his best friend in the city. 'Of course, if she had a daughter, I would marry her and look after all the property myself,' he would joke. 'I would take care of that imbecile son of hers too.'

Dino would smile, but never allow the joke

to stretch on. And he would wonder, about the daughter...

As he stood in front of the woman now, it suddenly struck him that she must be hardly five feet tall. And yet, Dino always felt small in front of her. He felt that everybody looked small and insignificant in front of her. Everybody except, of course, his elder brother, Sri Sri Dayananda Debo Goswami, the spiritual head of the Barbari *xattra*. Kuxumpriya Baruani baideo was his disciple.

~

His elder brother, whom he called *Dangor da*, had founded the religious institution at Barbari on his own, having cut himself off from their original xattra in Gohepara. By the time Dino was old enough to go to school, Dangor da had already left the parent xattra, and ever since, Dino had grown up hearing about his exploits. In local lore, just as in Dino's mind, his elder brother had become something of a legend. Tall tales were told of the vagabond *goxai*—the god among men—who moved from district to district, giving refuge to whole communities of converts and setting up branches of his own xattra. Their father, the old or *bura goxai*, had set up just one house of God in his lifetime, but Dangor da already had three. And even though he did not have a xattra in Guwahati, he had as his disciples some of the richest, most aristocratic families in the city, who often arrived at his remote xattras looking for spiritual guidance in their dust-covered motor cars.

Many years ago, on one rare occasion, when Dino had gone to Dangor da's Barbari xattra, Kuxumpriya baideo had come looking for the goxai. Morning prayers had just been concluded and the disciples had left for their homes. Dino and a few other boys were playing a game, running in and out of the prayer hall. Suddenly, there was a commotion outside the xattra and one of Dangor da's disciples, Ramani *bhakat,* had rushed in to announce the arrival of the lady with the delicately poetic name: Kuxumpriya, Dino recalled from a poem they had studied in school that year, meant 'beloved of flowers'.

He had run out to the road with the other village children just in time to see the woman who bore the name alighting from her once-white-now-grey-with-dust Premier Padmini. Dressed in a white *mekhala-sador* radiant with metallic gold motifs, she had looked like a queen to him, quite formidable, nothing delicate or flower-like about her. Then, when this royal personality had entered the *namghor* and bowed before his own brother, touching his feet, seeking his blessing, Dino had felt as if his heart would burst with pride.

It had taken a while for the awe to settle down and give way to curiosity. When it did, Dino had studied her entourage. It comprised of two ladies in waiting and a young girl, about Puni *bai's* age. For a brief moment, his heart ached for his elder sister who had been the one person in the family to make him feel loved. Without her sunny presence, he felt

abandoned. The girl seated on the namghor floor now
was nothing like his sister; she looked pale and sickly,
and distinctly uncomfortable.

One of the two ladies sat directly behind baideo,
fanning her with an intricately woven bamboo fan.
The other fussed over the folds of the girl's mekhala-
sador, ironing the pale pink silk between her fingers.
When she wasn't doing that, she was wiping the
sweat beads off the girl's forehead with a matching
pink handkerchief. Dino could make out from the
tormented look on the girl's face that she did not enjoy
any of this. She kept pushing away the attending lady's
hands and tugging at her sador, pulling it closer around
her body. If she was married, she could have covered
herself from head to toe, wrapping the loose end of
the long sador over her head like Kuxumpriya baideo
did. And if she did, Dino felt, she would become a
heap of silver flowers floating, gleaming on a stretch
of pink silk. The perfect offering for the goxai.

The girl kept stealing looks at the children who
were leaning in from every available window in the
namghor, pushing and shoving against each other
in their eagerness to witness the ceremony being
performed inside. Like them, Dino too could not
make head or tail of what was happening between
bhakatani, goxai and god in the sanctum sanctorum.
Being the youngest of four sons, he was not expected
to take over his father's xattra. And so, he remained
as yet uninitiated. Nobody really bothered with him
when it came to imparting the familial knowledge,

traditions and rituals of the xattra institution. Besides, he was the first among all the bura goxai's sons to complete primary schooling and go to middle school. His teacher, Khonin *mastor,* said he had high hopes for Dino and had even made a strong supplication to his father to allow the youngest heir to go for higher education whereby he could spread the glory of the xattra far and wide through the written word. Strangely enough, the bura goxai had agreed. Dino would be leaving for Patkusi soon to enrol in the high school there. Dangor da had arranged for his stay with one of his disciples at Patkusi.

Dino had no idea about what to expect once he left Gohepara. But he was excited. Dangor da had summoned him only yesterday to tell him that if he could complete high school, he would make arrangements for Dino to go to Guwahati! As he sat facing his elder brother in front of the *monikut,* the sanctum sanctorum of the prayer hall, Dino had suddenly felt something akin to filial affection towards him: as though his brother was a benign patriarch, and he, a beloved son. All his life, he had only known awe and amazement towards this man. Now that he felt an almost earthly sentiment creeping into his heart, it gave him, at the same time, a nagging sense of guilt. Dangor da was above such human affections; he was, like their father, a god among men—to be adored, but with admiration; to be worshipped and held in awe.

The kind of awe he now saw Kuxumpriya Baruani baideo holding him in, clinging to his every word, following every instruction in performing the ongoing ritual, bowing to his commands. The girl who came with her, however, seemed more interested in what was going on outside.

'Little mother, what is your name?'

Dangor da had to repeat his question before the woman attending to the girl shook her by her feet. 'Tell *goxai-deu* your name!' she said in a whisper loud enough for everybody to hear.

'Tejassini Barua,' she blurted out loudly, caught off guard.

Dangor da turned his back to her then and continued chanting the benedictions, uttering her name every now and then.

Dino liked the name, although he did not know what it meant. He wanted to know more about her and wondered if she was Kuxumpriya baideo's daughter. Why was she so sad? Maybe he could talk to her. Would she talk to him? People from the city did not normally waste their time on village bumpkins like him.

But then he remembered he wasn't a village bumpkin, was he? He was the son of the *xatrradhikar* Sri Sri Gopalsandra Debo Goswami, and the younger brother of Sri Sri Dayananda Debo Goswami. How could *he* be considered a bumpkin? He was not like these common village boys at all. It was beneath him, the little god—*kon goxai*—to be thus aligning himself with these lesser mortals. What was he doing peeping in through the window anyway? If he wished, he could go sit by his brother and offer the same benedictions. Why was he demeaning himself this way?

As the thought started gripping his mind and growing, Dino found himself grinding his teeth silently. He turned away from the window, but stopped short. For two brief seconds, his eyes clashed and held with the girl's. They were empty. Puni bai's eyes always reminded him of the *doyar xagor*—oceans of kindness—that the hymn talked about. And he loved how much love they held for him, always. But without understanding why, this girl's eyes surprised him with their barrenness.

As he walked out of the xattra towards the road, a strange sadness started descending upon Dino. He started feeling very heavy. It was as if, suddenly, his shoulders could not carry the weight of his being; he felt bogged down by dark clouds of immense sorrow. Of late, he had felt that happening to him more and more often. When it did, all he wanted to do was crawl into a corner and cry.

Just then, though, surrounded by so many people, he could not. So he sat under the *bokul* tree a little distance away from the xattra entrance. After a short while, the rituals must have ended for the crowd started slowly moving out of the namghor courtyard. From his vantage point, Dino saw Dangor da and Kuxumpriya baideo come out of the namghor and walk towards the pond in the backyard. They were deep in conversation. Dino's heart suddenly started beating faster. He saw a few boys from the village

approach the car and begin to draw faces and ugly
sceneries on its dusty bonnet with their fingers. His
heart filled with trepidation as he watched, from his
safe distance, the boys' grand act of subversion. What
would happen when the city lady finished conferring
with Dangor da? He sat there dreading that any
minute now the driver of the car would come charging
at them with a stick.

That did not happen, however, and when
Kuxumpriya Baruani baideo and her entourage had
finally driven off, leaving their hair white with dust,
Dangor da had explained to the naughty village boys
that being aristocratic also meant being large of heart;
but the next time they defaced any of his disciples'
cars, they would have to deal with him. Dino had
been glad he hadn't joined the boys earlier.

~

Many years later, when he had moved to Guwahati
to enrol in Cotton College, he had realised the truth
in Dangor da's words about aristocracy and large-
heartedness. For the first few months, he had lived in
a room with bamboo walls and a thatched roof that
let the rains in and dampened his bed, his clothes,
and worst of all, his books. He had spent many nights
awake, worrying that the thin plastic covering he had
retrieved from the roadside behind his college would
fail to protect his books from the heavy rains. His
clothes he could dry out the next morning over the
kerosene stove his landlady had so graciously provided.

He didn't mind that they would stink of kerosene for days afterwards: he never noticed how his classmates sniggered. But he could not allow the destruction of his books, bought with the money he earned from giving tuitions to the sons and daughters—some his own age—of the city's rich and famous.

Many of those whose houses he visited every evening to give tuitions—and also to save on his dinner expense—were disciples of his elder brother. They were extremely gracious to him and treated him with utmost respect, laying out clean *gamosas* for him and serving him food only in bell metal utensils. But he never allowed them to know about his predicament. Kuxumpriya baideo, though, heard about it one day from a disciple of Dangor da's who was delivering the goxai's benedictions to her in the city. She had immediately sent her chauffeur to seek him out and moved him to one of her own properties behind the hill.

Barua Asthan was a sizeable plot of land, next to the World War II Cemetery below the Nabagraha Hill. It was fenced and gated, with a small house in the middle. It had a tin roof and walls made of mud plastered over river rushes like most other houses in the city, except of course, of the very rich who had started moving into brick and mortar houses in recent years. His benefactress had been one of the first to do so.

As he drove him and his meagre possessions to the house, the chauffeur informed Dino that he had heard that baideo used to live in the same house when her husband was alive. He had died six years ago, leaving her with an infant son, born late in life.

'He's retarded, you know,' the driver whispered, loudly, as is proper when revealing a secret.

'And her daughter?' Dino asked, suddenly remembering those empty eyes, from what? Was it six or seven years ago now?

'She has no daughter,' the driver answered, his tone patient. Obviously, the village boy knew nothing about the family.

Dino felt embarrassed he had even asked. He had assumed that the girl who had accompanied Kuxumpriya Baruani baideo to Barbari was her daughter. He had been so sure. He ground his teeth now, silently, angry for having made a fool of himself. He decided to ride the rest of the distance in silence. The chauffeur, however, talked ceaselessly, pointing out the various landmarks of the city. Dino kept making appropriate noises of acknowledgement and gratitude at timely intervals, letting the chauffeur presume he was new in town.

When they reached Barua Asthan, Dino found that the house had been divided into three units to be rented out. Dino had been given a room on the cemetery side. The room in the middle was occupied by a high school teacher, Tarinikanta Deka. They were to share everything—the makeshift kitchen constructed in the back verandah as well as the bathroom; and beyond that, they also shared the same love of literature and writing. They bonded within a very short time over long evenings spent discussing books and making dire predictions about the future of Axamiya literature. The third unit, on the far end, comprised of two rooms and the main kitchen and bathroom. It had apparently been vacated some time back and new tenants were expected soon. But for as long as Dino lived there, the new tenants never came, and that portion of the house remained locked up.

Barua Asthan was further away from Dino's college than his earlier place, but Dino did not mind the long walk. It gave him a chance to meet and greet a lot of people along the way, and to observe life in the city closely. He had started writing stories for a few local tabloids and weekly newspapers: he found that it was a good way to earn some extra money. Of course, he wrote under a pseudonym for he did not want anybody in his family, or any of the xattra disciples for that matter, knowing how the youngest goxai wrote candidly about the material life in the city or about the youthful desires that its pale lights ignited in the restless hearts of lonely souls. He also wrote under an assumed name because he wasn't entirely sure he should indeed be writing on such subjects: he *was*, after all, the goxai's son, a little god himself, who should instead be contemplating upon spirituality and the deeper meanings of life.

But ever since coming to the city, Dino had found himself getting more and more intrigued by the sheer carnality that hid itself in the unlit crevices of the city.

The city was growing on him, day after day, month after month. He wanted to hate it, and maybe he did hate it too, but it would not leave him be. Like a living organism, it seeped into his soul, assaulted his senses, captivated his sensibility, till he did not know what it was he hated more: the city that would not let him be, or himself, who could not remain content with who he was born to be.

'Goxai, you worry too much,' Tarinikanta would chide him. He was the only one who knew Dino's secret and also the reader of his first drafts. 'You are going to be a great writer one day, and that is all that should matter to you. That is your destiny. Not the xattra for you, my friend—that is your Dangor da's destiny—but the annals of our living literary tradition.'

'It is sleaze, Tarini, sleaze. That is what I write. It is not literature,' in his dark moments, Dino would lament. 'Where I come from, we talk of love and surrender, not lust and gruesome death. We talk of crossing over from this world to the next, not getting caught in the web of fancy woven by those that know not the Most High!'

'My friend, as your critic, counsellor and champion, let me tell you this: I see you rising above it all, like the lotus that blooms in the mud. You shall overcome.'

Dino was not so sure.

And then, just last month, a publishing house of some repute had approached him through one of the tabloids he wrote for and requested a manuscript of his unpublished stories. Dino had started writing then, furiously, determined to live up to his friend's predictions. He had been given a chance and he had to be the lotus that bloomed in the mud. Being summoned to the big house had come as an irritant, but now that the flowers had spoken to him, maybe there was a story there too. The flowers had reminded him of a tale he had heard one day as a little boy, of a young girl who had grown into a plant, blossomed into a flower, become a lotus...

~

At their xattra, it had always been tales from the scriptures that one heard. But that day, he had heard Ramen *kaka's* mother telling her grandchildren the tale of an unfortunate girl killed by her stepmother.

Puni bai had been unwell and had sent him to Ramen kaka's house to fetch a homeopathic medicine he had brought for her from Guwahati. She had cautioned him to be very careful not to let anybody at the xattra or in the village know about it. If they found out the daughter of the *Xattradhikar* Sri Sri Gopalsandra Debo Goswami was ingesting medicine prepared by doctors from the city, she would be excommunicated; or worse still, made to go through all those excruciating cleansing ceremonies again.

Dino had been cautious for his sister's sake, making his way to Ramen kaka's house in the pitch darkness without a lamp. When he reached kaka's courtyard, he found the entire family huddled around a fire. When kaka saw him at the *nangala mukh*, he quickly stood up: 'Come in, come in, kon goxai. Come and have a seat inside.'

Dino enjoyed being the son of the spiritual leader of the community: it made him feel important, especially since even the elders called him a god. He always got special treatment in people's houses, and that included being made to sit separately from other children. But today he would have much preferred to sit around the fire with Ramen kaka's children and listened to Golapi *abu's* stories. As he waited for kaka to wrap the medicine in a piece of old newspaper, he heard the old woman's voice drift in through the thinning mud walls that were letting the light from the fire filter into the house, here and there, piercing through its bamboo skeleton. She had just started a new story, something about a girl named Tejimola.

Suddenly, Ramen kaka rudely interrupted everybody. He said in a raised voice from the threshold, 'Here, kon goxai, here is the new book I got for you from Guwahati.' Dino rose from the wobbly wooden bed he was seated on and held his right hand out. As his fingers closed around the newspaper wrapping, he ground his teeth silently. He mumbled something under his breath and started towards the nangala mukh.

As he passed the children huddled around the fire, though, his feet slowed down. He did not realise when they had stopped moving altogether, but there he was, listening to the saddest story he was to ever hear in his lifetime. The young girl, beautiful, so full of life, going to her friend's wedding and returning with her stepmother's silk clothes in tatters. The stepmother's feigned anger—for it was she who had hidden the mice in the folds of her own clothes that she had lent Tejimola—made Dino very angry. He moved closer to the fire and without knowing it, sat down.

'Eh, goxai's son! Hoh, don't sit on the ground; take this *pira*,' Golapi abu paused in her narrative long enough to scoop out the low wooden stool from under her buttocks and hand it to Dino. Nobody else said anything. Nobody else existed for them right now but the tragic little girl, tearful and terrified. Dino felt tears stinging his eyes when the stepmother ground Tejimola to death with a mortar and pestle and threw her remains in the backyard. Hope sprung up in his breast beating back the imminent tears when she grew into a fruit-bearing plant only to be cut down again. And then again, when she grew into a flowering creeper, and was cut down and thrown into the river. Dino thought his heart would burst with anger and fear and hope and joy and love and tenderness and he knew not what to name all those emotions he felt then as the old woman took her listeners on the rollercoaster ride of the wretched little girl's rising and falling fortunes until in the end, her lust for life triumphs. Overcoming multiple deaths, she floats finally on the river as a lovely lotus flower. Her father returning home by boat reaches out to pluck the flower and it sings out to him: 'Don't you reach out, do not pluck me...'

When the flower finally convinces the father: 'It is me, Teji', she returns to her old form. Dino remembered imagining a young girl rising up from the water, her tresses wet like Puni bai's after her morning bath, her thick white cotton mekhala-sador clinging to her as she trudges on her way to the riverbank. He also remembered feeling a sweet sadness that Tejimola's adventures were now over. He found no consolation in the stepmother's nose being cut off by the father, or her being banished to another land. All he could think about as he made his way back to the xattra that night, the contraband tied to his waist under the knot of his *dhuti*, was Tejimola's sad eyes as she emerged from the waters. He realised he could not discern what this sadness was all about: was it because even in death, she found no respite? Or was it, instead, because her post-human life adventures were now over? All he did know was that Tejimola's story affected him like no other.

And now, standing in front of his benefactress, looking into her eyes as each greeted the other with folded hands, his mind travelled back again to another pair of eyes, empty, lifeless. Who was she? Where *was* she? With uncharacteristic recklessness, Dino determined to find out.

~

'Where have you been hiding, kon goxai?'

The matriarch's tone was sharp, expressing a deep disappointment. She had sent her chauffeur to

summon him last week, but Dino had been unable to
tear himself away from his writing.

'Tell her I'll be there,' he had said and continued
writing.

He had not been attending college or going for his
tuitions as well. Tarini had tried to feed him his meals
a couple of times, but given up when he realised Dino
wanted to be alone with his writing.

'My friend, I shall not stand as the obstruction
in your path to greatness,' he had finally announced,
in his usual theatrical manner, and had withdrawn.

This morning, however, the chauffeur had banged
on his door again and offered to drag him bodily to
the big house, if required.

'Reach there by noon, or I will be back,' he had
threatened as he left.

Dino had shuffled around then, looking for his
sandals and making his way to the bathroom in the
backyard. He couldn't remember when he had last
bathed. He didn't want to bathe now; he felt his
stories might wash away with the bath water. But he
also knew that if he didn't take a bath, he would fall
into sin because Kuxumpriya baideo usually called
him to the house these days if she needed him to read
from the scriptures.

Dino did not know how much she knew about
his ignorance of the xattra rituals, but he thought
it best not to draw undue attention to it. He had a
strong voice, no doubt inherited from his father, and
he could sing well from the scriptures and that seemed

to suffice for his benefactress. Since she did not have a dedicated prayer room with a *monikut,* she would lay out a *thapona* instead and observe all the rituals around it in a practised manner: she had been Dangor da's disciple for a long time now. But since Dangor da could not come into the city very often, she had taken to calling upon his younger brother instead.

Kuxumpriya Baruani had taken refuge in the elder goxai, no doubt, but that did not mean that she could not berate his younger brother. She showed him all the reverence due to a member of the goxai's family, but was too used to the deference she herself received from everybody around her to allow a lesser god to disobey her diktat.

'Please accept my apologies, baideo. I wasn't hiding; I was writing. I have a manuscript due soon...' Dino's voice trailed away before the matriarch's direct gaze.

Suddenly, her eyes softened, and her whole body relaxed. She was a benign matriarch again, his benefactress.

'Good to know you are writing, kon goxai. You must tell me more about it.' But the finality in her tone did not indicate any real desire to know anything more about his writing ever, at all. Dino was relieved. He had blurted out his secret, without even realising it.

He followed her into the house and she indicated a chair which had a new gamosa spread out on it.

'Sit,' she said, softly.

Dino complied.

She lifted a curtain and walked out of the room through a door next to where Dino sat. For a long time, he could only hear distant voices and the faint clinking noises of utensils from behind the curtain, somewhere deep within the house. This was the first time Dino had been kept waiting. On the two or three earlier occasions that baideo had summoned him to her house, she had had the thapona ready on the floor in the far corner of the living room, the gamosa laid out over the rug that was to be his seat, and the holy book open at the page she wanted him to recite from. He would offer his prayers, recite from the book and when that was done, eat the food served to him there, on the floor. Baideo's maid would have packed some of the offerings for him in his bag by the time he was ready to leave. When he stood up to leave, both baideo and her maid would kneel on the floor and touch his feet. He would say a blessing, like he had seen his father and Dangor da do, and take a deep breath when he had finally turned his back on the house.

Today baideo did not need him to read from the book, and Dino suddenly felt a sense of panic wondering what it was that she did require of him. He sat there, feeling his heart palpitate, when there was a slight movement behind the curtain screening the door on the far wall from where Dino sat. Dino cleared his throat, thinking it might be the lady herself. But a little hand shot out from behind the curtain and drew it aside.

For the first time, Dino saw Kuxumpriya Baruani baideo's son. He was small for his age—and Dino had been told he was about six or seven. At first glance, he looked normal enough and Dino could not understand why everybody said there was something wrong with him. All Dino found different about him was that he wore a thick pair of glasses. They made his eyes look big and bulging.

When he emerged from behind the curtain, the little boy was smiling. The smile remained fixed on his face as Dino and he stared at each other from their respective positions, and neither of them moved for a long time. It was an innocent smile, but it disconcerted Dino. Finally he called out, 'Come here, babu. What is your name?'

The little boy moved forward slowly, cautiously, and when he was close enough, swiftly clambered up to Dino's lap and sat there with his head on Dino's chest, sticking his thumb in his mouth. Dino was taken aback. He did not know what to do.

'Are you sleepy?' he ventured. 'Shall I call your mother?'

The boy only shifted his head a little to study Dino's face. As he did so, his glasses were lifted from his eyes. Dino's breath suddenly left him as he found himself looking into a pair of eyes he had found clashing with his so many years ago at the Barbari xattra.

'Is he bothering you, kon goxai?' Kuxumpriya baideo walked in just then. She was followed by her maid who was carrying a tray laden with tea and snacks which she laid on the table next to Dino.

'Please help yourself, *goxai-deu*,' the maid said, and knelt before him, touching his feet. Dino muttered a prayer under his breath, touched his hand to her head and said, '*Hoise, hoise,* you can get up now.'

As the maid withdrew behind the curtain, Kuxumpriya Baruani lifted the little boy off Dino's lap. He went without protest. Dino's head was reeling, and he was having difficulty breathing. From somewhere far away, baideo's voice was floating in towards him.

'His name is Gungun, goxai. Everybody said I should not have a baby so late in life, that I should be ashamed of myself, but I couldn't kill an unborn child. Now look, he is paying the price for it...' the voice trailed away as Dino slowly started regaining his composure. He looked at the woman and child seated across the room from him. Gungun was curled up, quietly, in the ageing woman's lap the same way he had been in Dino's.

This woman seated in front of him now, was not the same formidable person who had met him at the front verandah not so very long ago. She looked frail. That gave Dino courage.

'And your daughter?' he asked.

Baideo looked up, startled. But she quickly regained her poise.

'So you remember her? I thought you might not. That would have been easier.'

Dino realised it was not proper to feel a sense of jubilation at such a moment, but he felt something akin to self-pride creeping into his heart as he waited for the old lady to elaborate.

In the same tired voice, she continued, 'She was ashamed of me, kon goxai. Her own mother! When she heard I was having a baby, she ran away from home. She left a note, you know, and she left. I haven't seen her since. Nobody remembers her. There was this engineer, a Gujarati boy, who had been following her around in college. She must have left with him. We do not talk about her anymore. It is best not to. She is dead to us...'

A tear escaped from behind her glasses. Dino felt very uncomfortable. He did not know if he should say something, but a deep sense of guilt or remorse or some other emotion he could not recognise just yet was rising in his throat and he could not speak.

'I had the baby prematurely, immediately after she left. My husband left us too, soon after. He was a good man, did a lot for the community. Everybody loved him. He died in his sleep one day, peacefully. He did not suffer,' baideo's voice trailed away.

Involuntarily, Dino took a deep breath. It made a deafening sound.

Baideo looked up from where she sat.

'Only Gungun and I were left behind, tied to each other by birth and death.'

Dino was afraid she might start crying again. That would be most embarrassing. Thankfully though, she just sat there, in front of him, head bowed again, in silence. The little boy sucked his thumb, his head tucked safely in baideo's bosom.

After a long time, the matriarch raised her head and looked directly at Dino.

'You will not discuss any of this with my servants though, will you? They are new and they do not know. I'm telling you all this because you are family. You deserve to know. Your Dangor da has been the greatest source of strength and succour for me through all this. You will keep my trust?'

Dino hastened to assure her he would never talk about any of this.

'You can trust me, baideo,' he said.

'Good then, have your tea. It's gone cold. Shall I have it heated for you again?' but she did not wait for him to respond and held the cup up for him.

Dino took the cup from her and sipped the cold tea.

'Now to business,' she announced, suddenly back to her old self. 'You must be wondering why I've called you here today?'

'I was...' Dino started, but she cut him short.

'I want you to tutor Gungun. Can you do that?'

It wasn't so much a question as a command, and Dino knew he'd have to do her bidding whether he wanted to or not.

'I'll pay you, of course...'

'No, no,' Dino started to protest, but she continued as though she had not heard him.

'You will come in every Saturday and Sunday for an hour in the morning, and teach him the alphabet and numbers to start with. I need to make sure that after I am gone, he can at least sign his name and do some basic calculations. I am not here forever, you know. Nobody is. So he is in your charge from now on.'

Dino realised he had been given his instructions and dismissed. He rose to leave, his heart heavy, fearful. He did not want to come to this house again, ever again, but he also knew he was being given no choice.

As he descended the few steps from the verandah into the driveway, making his way towards the gate, he found himself unable to look up. He did not want to see the flowers again, or hear their tale. He suspected he knew it already, but he did not want their tears to tell him, not now.

Thankfully the chauffeur was at the gate, just walking in.

'So you had to come down to earth finally, huh, goxai?' he smirked.

Dino only ground his teeth, not looking at him. And for the whole distance to his house, he kept his eyes directed to the ground, seeing nothing.

~

As his feet moved mechanically forward, a dark cloud glowered inside Dino's head, clogging his ears, damming his thoughts. He did not even realise when he had crossed the hill and reached the cemetery next to his house. But when he came to, he was seated on a gravestone. It was the same gravestone ('*Name Unknown, Pioneer, Indian Pioneer Corps, Death: 9/8/1945*' it read) he and Tarini had sat upon one evening, about ten days back, reading Nabakanta Barua's poetry. Tarini had brought them there to read the one about the dead moon rising from its grave. He had chosen the spot because it was secluded, situated at the far end of the cemetery where the land started undulating upwards, creating small hillocks that skirted around the Nabagraha Hill.

'Goxai,' Tarini had said, 'who needs alcohol when we have poetry to get drunk on?'

'*Hei, hei,*' Dino had chided him then. 'Don't talk about alcohol, Tarini, or we will fall into sin.'

'But you, a goxai from the xattra, are already deeply in sin, my friend,' Tarini had taunted, 'for you have entered the necropolis of the *boga bongal*, the white man, the foreigner, the *Christian*!'

Dino had walked away in a huff then, and not spoken to Tarini for a couple of days. His friend had wheedled his way back in, though, as he usually did. They were two people alone in a city that was not yet home. They only had each other.

Dino was startled to find himself there again. What was it that had dragged him back there, he wondered. And he felt afraid. He rose to leave but in his haste, dropped his bag. His stories spilled out. As he was collecting them, his hand brushed against the thorns of the Japanese rose bush that bloomed merrily on the grave of the unknown soldier. He felt his skin smarting. A thin red line appeared on the back of his hand. Droplets of blood.

'Tej,' the word snaked its way into his heart. It was icy cold.

Slinging the bag over his shoulder again, Dino climbed over the broken fence that separated Barua Asthan from the cemetery and hurried back to his room. He closed the door behind him and paced around the room. He sat on his bed, then jumped up. He thought he should empty his bag; check to see he had not lost any of his stories. His hands were shaking slightly when he reached in to retrieve the pages untidily tucked into the bag. A low terrified whimper escaped him when his fingers touched something fleshy inside his bag. He withdrew his hand and emptied the contents onto his bed. He almost laughed out loud when he saw a bunch of pale pink Japanese roses squished between the pages of his stories. And then he cried.

Dino cried and cried and cried. Hugging his knees to his chest, he sat on the floor, rocking back and forth. The tears wouldn't stop.

~

'Goxai, o goxai!' Tarini's voice woke him up, and the loud thumping on the wall next to his bed. The two of them were 'wall-mates'.

Dino sat up on his bed to see it was almost dark

outside. A bright orange sun was sending in the last of its warm rays into his room through the ventilator above the window. He sneezed a couple of times then, for the dust from Tarini's wall thumping was tickling his nose.

'Oh, so you are alive?' Tarini sounded angry. 'I have been trying to wake you up for the past half an hour. I was going to break the door next.'

'No need. I'm opening it,' Dino called out as he walked towards the door. His whole body was stiff. And he felt hungry. When Tarini appeared in front of his room, he asked, 'Do you have anything to eat?'

'I do. But what happened to you? What happened at the big house? What did the old woman want?'

'I'm hungry. Let's eat and then we can talk.'

If Tarini was put off by Dino's apparent calm, he did not say anything. He went back into his room and returned a little while later with two plates of boiled rice, some fish fry, salt and mustard oil.

'Let's eat in your room,' he suggested.

Dino was leaning against a pillar on the back verandah looking out at the many-hued sky that was slowly being devoured by the darkness of a moonless night. He followed Tarini back to his room.

His friend stopped short, without comment, when he saw the state of his stories, crushed under his weight while he had slept on top of them. Dino watched, motionless, as Tarini placed the food on one corner of the bed, picked up the pages from the bed, and ironing them with his hands, arranged them in a pile on the overcrowded table. Dino's heart beat fast when, suddenly, Tarini noticed the tiny bunch of pink roses on the floor beside the bed and bending down, picked them up and placed them on top of the pile.

When he was done with the pages, Tarini picked up the plates from the bed again. Dino almost snatched his plate from his friend's hand and started stuffing his mouth with large fistfuls of rice.

'What is this, goxai? What's happening to you? You must tell me.' Tarini's voice was shrill with concern.

'I don't know what to tell you,' Dino said, licking his fingers. 'Let's finish our food and then we can talk.'

Dino was stalling and Tarini knew it. But he said nothing.

After they had washed their dishes, they sat down on the bench in the front verandah like they did on most nights. Tarini shifted his weight a little to retrieve from the stained side pockets of his trousers a bunch of *tamul-paan* wrapped in soggy newspaper.

'I plucked them yesterday,' he said, perhaps hoping to start the conversation.

For a while, the two friends chewed their tamul-paan in silence. Then Tarini stood up to spit out the red juice that oozed out from chewing the mixture of betel nut, betel leaf and white lime. He miscalculated, and instead of falling on the ground below the verandah, most of the red juice was now splattered on the whitewashed pillar in front of them. Dino stared at the stain, and kept staring.

'So are you going to say something now?' Tarini tried again.

In some remote corner of his brain, the thought occurred to Dino that his friend's patience with him must have run out.

'She wants me to tutor her son,' he offered.

'He'll want more,' said a voice in the same remote corner of his brain.

'And that scares you? Why?' His friend was not to be fooled.

'I cannot lie to him. He's my only friend,' the voice threatened to break free of that precariously controlled zone inside his brain.

Out loud, he said, 'No, but being in that house does.'

'Why did I say that?' the voice inside him squealed.

'Why, goxai?' Tarini sounded genuinely surprised.

'I don't know,' Dino answered honestly. The voice in his head became quiet.

'Did you hear something? See something out of the ordinary? These big people have bigger secrets than their houses. Did she kill her husband or something, ha? She is a strong woman, she could've. Tell me, tell! I always thought it was convenient how he died so soon after the son was born. But then he died here, in this house, you know.'

'How old do you think she is, Tarini?' His friend's feverish outburst awakened something in Dino too and he was suddenly animated.

'Maybe around fifty?' Tarini sounded hopeful. Was this leading somewhere?

'That's not so old in some cultures, no?'

'No, fifty is not old,' said Tarini. The tone of Dino's voice had suggested he wanted some reassurance. 'But when a woman is married off at fifteen or sixteen, by the time she is forty, she has acquired all the trappings of old age. By fifty, she is ancient, I suppose.'

'Are you thinking about her son? Do you know something I don't? Is he not Xarbessar Barua's son? Whose bastard is he then?' Tarini persisted.

'I don't *know* anything,' Dino said and retreated again.

'*Shhhhhhhhhh…*' there was a soft hiss in his head. The picture of a wide-eyed toddler with a finger on his lips peered out at him from the mud wall of somebody's house. Dino was standing in front of a calendar without dates, studying the toddler in the semi-darkness. There was light flickering in from outside. An old woman was seated by the fire outside, telling the gruesome tale of the young girl with a lust for life, her name signifying the life-blood that flowed in her veins. Tej, Tejimola, Tejassini…

Somewhere far away, he heard Tarini sigh. He struggled to come back. He saw deep concern in his friend's eyes.

'Let's go sleep, goxai. You don't look so well,' he heard Tarini say. 'Do you want me to sleep in your room? Will you be all right?'

'No, no, Tarini, I'm fine,' Dino assured him. If his friend caught the feeble note in his voice, he did not react to it. Dino could feel the blood thumping in his veins again, threatening to cut out the air in his lungs.

'Well then, don't latch your door. I'll check in on you if I hear anything to worry me.' Tarini waited for Dino also to rise and let him walk ahead. Dino entered his room and shut the door behind him. Then, he heard his friend's footsteps receding.

~

When Dino woke up, nearly a month later, he could not at first remember what had happened in the long night that had followed. He felt weak and drained. But the memories had trickled back in, slowly.

Kuxumpriya Baruani baideo's chauffeur had driven him back to his room, uncharacteristically quiet. Dino was relieved. Ramani bhakat had his food ready and was waiting for him in his room. The bhakat had looked after him the past few days at the hospital.

'Ramani kaka, when do you leave? Dangor da will need you at the xattra,' Dino said between mouthfuls of rice.

'Your Dangor da needs me to be here, so here I am,' the bhakat said, simply.

Dino remembered how he had felt at first, seeing the lines of worry on Dangor da's forehead when he had come to visit him at the hospital.

'You are okay?' he had asked authoritatively when Dino had opened his eyes from his drug-induced sleep. One could almost miss the question mark at the end of his sentence.

'Dangor da,' Dino had whimpered, and he had wept again then, like he had wept for the many days and nights past, between his dreams of a young girl, whose mother had stopped loving her because her father would not. He loved her not as a father, but as a man who was not her father.

'Dino, what's happening to you? Stop crying like a girl!' Dangor da's voice was impatient, harsh. It stemmed the tide; he did not want to disappoint his brother.

How then could he tell him, or anybody else for that matter, that he did indeed feel like a girl, *that* girl, whose eyes had haunted him day and night; whose pain had left behind lacerations on his body and soul; whose life-blood had oozed out of *his* being; whose *tej,* indeed, was his tej.

'What is all this you have been blabbering about to your friend? You have scared him away.'

'Tarini is gone? Where?' Dino asked weakly.

'He got a job last week in Shillong. He left you at the hospital and ran away,' Dangor da said. 'I don't know if you will ever get a job yourself now. Mad people do not get jobs.'

Dangor da's tone hurt Dino. He felt like crying again, but controlled himself. Was he really mad?

'So this is what we are going to do now,' the god among men was taking charge. 'We tell everybody you had fever and delirium. You go prostrate yourself before Kuxumpriya, ask for her forgiveness. Then you pack your bags from her house and shift to Manabendra Goswami's outhouse. You sit for your exams and I'll see to it that you get a teaching job at

Patkusi. Oh, and stop writing nonsense. I have asked Ramani to burn your stories.'

Dino turned his face to the wall. He pretended to go back to sleep and did not acknowledge Dangor da when he called out to him a few seconds later that he was leaving.

Dino always knew that Dangor da had a huge following among the rich and the famous in Guwahati. Now he realised why. He solved their problems both in the spiritual realm and right here, on this soiled earth. He was a true leader of men, a god on earth. And he, Dino, was nobody, a mad man. Society was for normal people. In order to function in society, one would have to act normal, right, even if one was not quite that? Dino determined to follow Dangor da's instructions to the letter.

As he drifted off to sleep again, a little worm started crawling around inside his heart, nibbling its way around. He felt a mild pain and tears stung the inside of his eyelids. He stifled a sob trying to escape his throat. He remembered Puni bai's eyes, those oceans of kindness that had been his refuge throughout his childhood. It had been years now since he had revelled in her love. If only she had not eloped with that good-for-nothing Xorot, she could have come to visit him. Now she was an outcaste in the village. He would be too if he let her so much as touch him. He had wanted his elder brother to touch his hand to his forehead though, and bless him. Maybe if he had not pretended to fall asleep, he would have...

Dino did not want to live in Barua Asthan any longer than was absolutely necessary. He was frightened of the night for he remembered now that during the last few weeks, the nights had brought an endless stream of dreams. He had dreamt of Tejassini, lying on her bed, empty eyes pinned to the ceiling. He had dreamt of the heavy weight she had had thrust upon her, of being her father's daughter. Her father: a good man, who did a lot for the community; everybody loved him. And he loved her, night after night, day after day, until her mother hated her for it. His dreams had led him to wander out of his room to the part of the house where it had all happened, and which had remained locked, forbidding enquiry. Tarini had dragged him back to his room one night after he had woken up to hear his friend trying to break open the lock with a brick.

'Hei, hei, hei, goxai, what are you doing?' Tarini had come running down the verandah towards him. It had taken him an enormous amount of effort to lead Dino back to his room. Dino had resisted, suddenly discovering strange reserves of inhuman strength in himself but Tarini had always been bigger and stronger than him. For the rest of the night, he had had to be physically restrained. At one point, Tarini had even threatened to tie him to the bed with a rope; only, he could not get himself to do that to his friend. His eyes had shone with sheer horror as he had sat through the night listening to Dino's ramblings.

'He got what he deserved, Tarini, I'm telling you,

he got what he deserved...But she should have loved her. Why didn't she love her?'

By the time the sun rose in the morning, Dino had dozed off. He had woken up some time later to find Tarini nodding his head in an uncomfortable sleep, perched on the wooden chair next to his bed. His friend had sat vigil throughout the night.

The mornings had been lucid, Dino remembered. And they had brought with them shame and guilt. He had woken Tarini up then and asked him to go sleep on his own bed. Tarini had refused.

'You will drive me mad too, goxai!' he had complained. 'All night I heard your tales of Tejimola dead in childbirth, blossoming back to life, and of purple flowers weeping tears of blood over the gate in the big house. I get what her name means: *kuxum-priya*. What's that got to do with *tej*, Tejimola, bloody murder?'

Dino had felt shame wash over him in waves as his friend had continued in a petulant voice, 'I blame myself, goxai. I should have seen the signs and steered you away. But I was in the throes of my own theatrics about you as this mad genius, this creative genius. You need to give your mind some rest. I will take you to the hospital today. Will you come?'

Dino had gone without protest, and Tarini had never returned. His friend's desertion seemed well deserved to Dino now, but at the hospital, he had had the most gruesome dreams about his fate. He had, after all, promised to be back the next day after he had sent word home through Kuxumpriya Baruani.

'Don't tell her I know,' his parting words to his friend had come out slurred. The drugs were already having their sedative effect...

As he packed his meagre belongings and piled them on to a rickshaw with Ramani bhakat's help that evening, he wondered what or how much of his ramblings Tarini had indeed relayed to the matriarch. He guessed from Dangor da's involvement that he must have revealed some of the details, and he dreaded the moment next morning when he would have to be face to face with his former benefactress, taking her leave, asking her forgiveness, as instructed. But he was determined to go through with it, to face his demons, and to emerge victorious.

Dino felt an electric sense of renewal and rejuvenation as he walked down to Kuxumpriya Baruani baideo's house the next morning. He remembered the many cleansing ceremonies he had witnessed in the xattra growing up and realised that in some ways, he was going through one of them himself. He was, after all, purging his past, and cleansing his soul of the dark and dreadful thoughts that had poisoned him to the point of madness.

He felt ecstatic and he walked briskly.

He was almost at the house now, and he stopped short.

There was new construction underway. The rickety old iron gate was gone. A small muddy path, wide enough for one person to pass by at a time, had been left in the centre of what used to be the gate earlier.

And on either side of this path, were two deep gaping holes. Sturdy iron rods embedded in a cement base were sticking out of the holes.

The creeper was gone. The flowers were gone. Tejassini-Tejimola was gone.

Dino turned around hastily and started walking back. He had to reach the river.

THE NURSE

Janice Pariat

It had been months now since he'd touched her. And she'd forgotten what it felt like, skin on skin.

The roughness of fingertips. The pincer clench of arms.

At the beginning, it hadn't been like this. Or let's say it hadn't been this bad.

Because, honestly, she couldn't have ever called him 'cuddly'. Or—what was that awful phrase?— touchy-feely. She'd wondered whether perhaps he'd never been hugged in childhood. That's what she'd read, anyway, on a website, found after she tentatively Googled 'boyfriend not cuddly'. (Embarrassing, but she didn't know how to phrase it more eloquently.) With some trepidation she'd clicked on the first result, uncompromisingly called '12 Things You Need To Know About Dating A Partner Who Doesn't Show Affection'. Surely it wasn't that dire? In bold, phlegmatic font, it began: *Partners who don't show an abundance of affection to their significant others are typically Thinking (T) types on the Myers–Briggs Type Indicator.*

She had no idea what that meant.

But she'd read on, diligently.

And made a few discoveries.

That he probably viewed the world, and relationships, from a logical, impersonal perspective, that one night of snuggling would have to last her several weeks, that a hand placed on her leg 'meant a lot', that she could forget about long, heartfelt discussions about their feelings, that if she forced her love on him he'd most probably feel overwhelmed and stifled. All this stemmed, the author seemed convinced, from the fact that he hadn't been hugged in childhood.

Terribly annoying, of course, this.

And she'd had fantasies of chiding his parents. This is what wanton lack of familial love and attention has made of your son.

He was a robot.

Despite all this she didn't break up with him or call it off. She told herself it was because, despite having been abandoned before, by friends and lovers, yes mostly lovers, it wasn't the sort of thing she would do. That despite being an abandonee, she wasn't an abandoner. Also, she thought, most secretly, that she could save him.

That through their bond, special and unique, he would change.

They'd met, or rather re-met, at a friend's birthday party. She'd just moved back to the city after being away for years, and he happened to be in town. Had it really been—they counted in amazement—twelve years? Since they'd left university, where he'd studied History and she English Literature. Not that they'd hung out with the same people; he was heavily involved with student union politics and standing for college presidential elections, while she was busy with the drama society, and music. It became a joke between them—he the serious one, and she the hippie stoner.

Except he was the one who flunked their last year.

'Too busy saving the world,' she'd tease.

And he'd protest saying their college needed to introduce a more lenient class attendance policy.

At the beginning, it was sweet.

The playfulness, and calls, the midnight messaging and morning texts. He lived a few hours away from the city, in a hill town where he taught at a boarding school, and over his winter vacation—their first winter together—he stayed in the city, and they met, often, voraciously, delighting in each other's company. Meeting for lunches, going for plays, and spending lost hours in bed. He made her laugh. His attentiveness touched her like a rare, gentle song.

Life felt transformed.

But even then she noticed, that apart from sex, they wouldn't touch.

And even after sex, the intimacy was minimal. He'd place a desultory hand around her for a while, and then take it away. They wouldn't spoon.

Soon enough, when she thought they'd grown less formal with each other, she'd playfully demand, 'Hold me!' or tease 'Rolling over and falling asleep, are we?'

He'd laugh and say, 'I'm not a cuddler...'

'No,' she'd kiss him on the nose, 'you're a prickly pear.'

She supposed it didn't loom as an issue then because the sex was good. A special, resolute chemistry. He knew what to do, and when, and how. And no matter how many times the moves were repeated, as these things tend to be over time, she didn't tire of it, and as far as she could tell, neither did he. He liked her on top. She liked being below. But they found compromises, taking generous turns satisfying each other.

Even when he left at the end of winter, they continued.

Long distance.

And because it wasn't all that far, and she was willing and ready to travel, they managed, and managed well. When they met, after two or three weeks apart, it was all tongue and touch and breathlessness. So, sex wasn't the problem. It was touch beyond that. The strict no public display of affection policy he implemented. 'I can't do that here,' he explained, 'too many people know me.' She didn't bring up how even in the city, a city of sixteen million, he wouldn't hold her hand, or place an arm around her. How when they were in a room together, he strictly occupied his own space.

That's it, she thought. He has a strong sense of his own.

A friend told her how perhaps they spoke different languages of love.

'What does that mean?'

That people, her friend explained, have different primary ways of showing each other they care. Some give gifts, to let you know they're thinking of you at a particular time and place. The gift, in some way, is a tangible symbol of affection, because it's been picked with you in mind.

Some offer acts of service. They will cook for you, and drop you off to work, and make sure there's always milk in the fridge.

Others may talk. The sharing of stories and emotions. They will *tell* because, for them, words are affirmation. Expect to hear that you are wonderful. That, to them, you mean an awful lot. Support will come in the form of verbal expression. To hear is to know it's real.

('That's not really his love language,' she remembered thinking.)

The other involves time. Together. Not watching a movie or a TV show, but giving each other undivided attention. Switching off devices, and looking at each other and talking. Going for a walk, just the two of them, or a meal.

And finally (she held her breath), touch. To communicate emotional love through physical gestures. A caress on the shoulder as you pass through a room. An unexpected kiss. To embrace when you leave, and when you return. It is wordless yet speaks volumes. That's it, she remembered thinking, this is mine. It's the way I understand love.

At first, for him, she settled on gifts.

He gave her an abundance. A bookmark, books, a pair of woolly Tibetan socks. A handmade paper notebook. A carefully chosen scarf. Then, over the months, those too, dwindled. To words—'I'll get it for you' or 'Next time, I'll pick it up for you' or 'I must get you this'—and she slowly almost stopped believing him because the gifts didn't come. Or came infrequently. And with much, it seemed, deliberation.

Then she thought how he might speak the language of service. He was attentive, sometimes to a fault. Opening doors for her, and making sure she'd always be picked up and dropped off at the airport when she made her journeys to see him. She'd get tea in bed. And a meal waiting whenever she arrived. But, her friend asked, isn't that just…good manners? Or being hospitable? Wouldn't he do that for anyone who came to visit? Perhaps, she conceded, but told herself silently that it was because he cared, that he'd do these things for her and only her.

The trouble started over the summer.

He'd had a busy term at school, many family house guests dropping by and staying for extended visits, a bout of illness. She didn't know whether it was all that that finally made him snap. The place where she worked in the city was also on vacation, and she thought it would be nice to stay with him longer. That finally, it wouldn't just be a weekend that they spent together. A lovely but rushed sliver of time that was always over almost as soon as it had begun. This would be different. They'd get 'quality time' together. She envisioned long summer evenings on the lawn, talking, reading, going for walks. Waking up with the knowledge of not having to leave that day or the next. For once, they'd get to do what 'normal' couples did, the ones that lived in the same place.

It was in this spirit that she packed in a bigger suitcase this time, throwing in more clothes, more underwear, more sandals. He was there when she was packing, and she wondered whether it was only in hindsight that she thought he looked perturbed. But it wasn't the thought to indulge—that your lover didn't want to spend as much time with you as you did with him. And so they left for the hills. Away from the dry heat and dust of the city. He seemed a little distant, but she thought it was because he was tired.

On the flight, he held her hand through the turbulence.

Her heart was as elated as the clouds.

When they got to his place, they stayed in bed most of the afternoon until the early evening. At the dinner party they attended at a friend's house, he kissed her on the forehead when she said something sweet. The place was dimly lit and swirling with people high on smoke and alcohol, but she remembered the feel of his hands wrapping for a few seconds around her cheeks, how he leant closer. He loves me, she remembered thinking. He loves me.

A few days later, he snapped.

It wasn't their first fight. They'd tussled over things

in the past; the time he had to cancel plans with her because of work, the time she forgot to book dinner reservations for New Year's Eve. But this was strangely big.

It was mid-morning. She came downstairs, notebook in hand, thinking she'd do some work. Then she caught a glimpse of him in his study. Feet up, smoking, watching a movie on his laptop.

'Hey,' she called playfully, walking up to him. 'Why didn't you ask if I wanted to watch a movie with you?' She jabbed him lightly on the arm.

He shouted back, 'Because I told you I wanted time on my own.'

If the day had been peacefully quiet until then, it was painfully silent now. The quality of it changed. She stepped back, in surprise, then shock.

'What do you mean...I only...' she managed to stammer.

'I told you, didn't I?'

'Told me what...?'

'That I wanted to be on my own for a bit.'

She admitted he had. At one point, in the city, when he was over at her apartment, telling her how it had been so hectic, and that he was looking forward to some alone time. Except she hadn't understood he considered her too an...intrusion. That her being in his house was an inconvenience he had to reckon with.

'I wasn't even going to join you,' she said, suddenly defensive. 'I was just teasing...'

'No, you meant it...I know you meant it.'

She sat on the sofa, feeling like she couldn't stand or move.

'See...and this has happened...when all I wanted was some quiet...now the morning's ruined.'

It felt like a slap. Sharp and stinging across her face.

'I'm sorry,' she mumbled, 'I didn't know...'

'Yes, you did,' he said. Lighting up another cigarette. 'You knew but you chose to ignore what I told you.'

He was right, she supposed. Technically.

But wasn't this the point? To learn how to be separate even while together? Wasn't that how people built a relationship, a life?

'I'll leave you alone...' She fumbled with her slippers, her book.

'Yes, but look at the mood we're in now...'

She fled upstairs. And cried in the bathroom.

He was right; it was her fault. She was the bad listener. The selfish one. The one who'd only wanted to do what *she* wished to do. After a while of sitting on the toilet seat, staring blankly at the tiles white and cold beneath her feet, she decided. This is what she'd do. This is what she'd tell him.

By the time she went downstairs again, lunch had been laid out. He was just about to call her, he said. They ate in near silence, but he seemed calmer. When they were finished and he picked up a book and settled on an armchair, she told him she was leaving. 'I'll book a place in L—' she said, 'and stay there a few days.'

'Are you crazy? That'll be like I'm booting you out of the house...'

She stayed silent.

'No, I can't allow you to do that.'

She fought plaintively; it'll be better, she said. She'd rather be there than here. Where she was unwanted, she completed in her head.

'Don't be silly,' he chided. And the matter, at least for him, was settled.

She stumbled back upstairs. Into the bedroom in the furthest, quietest corner of the house and flopped miserably on the bed.

He didn't want her to leave. He didn't want her to stay.

It was confounding.

She watched the light outside change, as the sky darkened.

At some point, he walked into the room, lay beside her and read. Maybe it was his way of saying their fight was over? That she was forgiven for her terrible oversight.

A few days later she left, and travelled back to the city. This time she took the train. And the departure felt all that more extended. A prolonged execution of separation. They hadn't even made plans when they'd meet again; she'd been afraid to bring it up. It wasn't ideal, at this point, to speak of reunions.

And she supposed it was after those few days, the fights that continued long into the night, and began first thing in the morning, that things changed in the times they met thereafter. The sex, though still good, diminished too.

And the touching, well, the touching only happened on the rarest occasions.

Which, in a strange way, made her treasure it even more.

She was like a child, waiting to be rewarded for good behaviour.

If she behaved as he wanted her to, if she were obedient and appropriate, she would receive a stray kiss on the forehead.

It made her unbelievably happy.

She had to earn it, she told herself. It became something she had to deserve. Not freely given, it gained more value. She craved it, of course, looking to sit close to him on the sofa, to stand near him at dinner parties. To be in his proximity. Always on the lookout for a gesture from him to prove he still loved her. That yes, he wanted her there.

Then she fell ill.

A strange persistent fever that struck in the middle of the night.

The next morning, when he awoke and looked at her flushed, feverish face, he asked, in some alarm, 'What happened? Are you okay?' She mumbled a reply, unable to open her eyes. 'Not feeling so good.'

'What happened, baby?' (He hadn't called her that in months, at least not since their fight over the summer.)

'Feeling feverish...'

He touched her forehead, then clasped her to him. 'We'll go see a doctor.'

And he tended to her as the tenderest lover would. Bringing her tea, and touching her arm, sitting by her on the bed. It was wondrous.

By the second day, when she was visibly better, the affection dropped. She was almost disappointed to have recovered so quickly.

The next time, a few weeks later, she was in the city.

She texted him saying his superstar (what he called her, or used to, in fondness) wasn't well.

A barrage of messages followed. 'You must get tested, baby.' 'Shall I have a car sent for you to take you to the doctor?'

In the middle of the day, he called to ask how she was feeling. And that was a miracle, because they hardly spoke on the phone anymore. Their every-night calls had dwindled to once every four or five days, and she'd consoled herself by saying that's what always happened; relationships can't thrive at the same level of intensity. Passions transform to mundane comfort. Things settle. But she still missed it, of course, their daily catch-ups, that she felt were necessary to make them feel connected. On the days she was ill though, he checked on her often. Sometimes, first thing in the morning. She was unwell, but for the first time in ages, happy.

The next month when she had some time off and visited him, she knew it was bad timing. He was in the midst of organising a school event, a conference involving hundreds of participants. She tried to be supportive, to be cheerful and encouraging.

To be, and at this she tried so hard, less demanding. To not expect him to be able to spend time with her, and then be surprised and overjoyed when he did. If I fall sick, it will be different, she remembered thinking.

And, to her amazement, she did.

A complicated UTI, that required her to conduct blood tests and CAT scans, and eventually take two different types of antibiotics. He was most concerned, and most attentive.

He arrived early from work, sat at her bedside, caressed her face to check for fever, kissed her forehead. She was so happy she hoped the infection would last long. And it did, for a week. Which she spent with him, and slowly recovered.

It was funny. How willing herself to fall ill usually worked.

She wondered whether it was a special gift she had. This thinking of a fever at bedtime, and waking up with one in the morning.

To will an upset stomach.

A throat infection.

An inexplicable rash.

But she didn't do it every time she visited because then it might seem suspicious.

One weekend a month, out of the two she spent with him, seemed to do the trick. They wouldn't have sex while she was unwell, but everything else made up for it.

She lost weight but she felt loved.

Then as all things do, this too began to wear off. He seemed to tire of it. These frequent spells of illness. Slowly, it became as before. Everything, she realised with alarm, could be normalised. What could she do? If this couldn't keep him by her side—rather, her bedside—she needed to find something else. It was tricky. What degree of illness could she conjure at will? What if she didn't recover and died?

The answer came one evening as they sat and watched a TV show together in his study. He was on a wooden stool, smoking; she sat on his leather writing chair, one that tipped far to the back, but he promised would never fall over. Except when she leaned back, it did. She hit her head on the floor, and her hand, caught in the arm of the chair, twisted. When she opened her eyes, he was looking down at her, concern drawn across his face.

The same kindly questions. 'Are you okay? Are you hurt?'

Her hand was swelling, colouring into an ugly bruise, and the back of her head would be sore for days. He put his arms around her and picked her up, placing her on the sofa. She almost fainted from pain, and joy.

Every once in a while, then, she would fall.

Take a tumble.

Slip on a stair.

Crush her fingers in a car door.

Cut herself while chopping fruit. He would

patiently clean, and wrap, and bandage. Rolling crepe around a twisted ankle, applying warming gel on a sore back muscle. She would close her eyes, and try and capture the feel of his fingertips on her skin. His closeness. He loved her. She was sure of it, he loved her.

But she could also see that it had to slowly increase in degree. A sprain would no longer suffice, it had to be a burn (accidentally setting the tea cloth on fire and letting it touch her skin). A nick on her finger had to swell to a deep, dangerous cut (a serrated bread knife did the trick). A slip on a step needed to proceed to a fall from the top of the flight of stairs.

At night, often, she would catch herself crying. She couldn't do this anymore. She was running out of ideas. And then he would leave her. He would have no reason to stay, to care for her, to nurse her back to health.

Unless, she thought, one glimmering sleepless dawn, it was terminal.

Something that would last always. That offered, for her, no hope of recovery.

But how could she possibly manage that? She hadn't conjured up an illness in a long while. Could she still do it? Would it work? She fell asleep fitful and restless.

The next day, she took a walk while he was away at work. He came home late these days. Then he freshened up, sat in front of his laptop, spoke barely a few words to her, ate dinner, and then, in exhaustion, fell asleep. He did seem very tired. And he mentioned often how he felt fatigued to the bone. She didn't know if this was true, or whether they were excuses to get out of having sex, being affectionate, spending quality time with her. It was hopeless. His silence was killing her anyway. So this, she supposed, was her only hope.

It would have to be something slow and extended, so he would be hers longer.

Nothing that would act swiftly. She ran through options in her mind. What would she choose? It was precarious, a balance between life and death. She didn't want too much pain because the medication would be strong, and then how would she enjoy his company?

On the road, she stopped at a pharmacy, a small, old shop whose shelves burst with boxes of all shapes and sizes. How much they could cure. How much they couldn't heal. Which one of these would she end up taking?

She walked back to his place resolute that that night she would conjure it, the last illness.

The one that would linger.

It came to her, the disease, as she turned into the gate.

Suddenly, her heart lightened. She had decided, and with her decision things seemed simple, clear. Like the sky above her, coloured an unbelievable mountain blue.

That day she did all the things she liked to do. She cooked a nice meal, did some gardening, laid out seeds and breadcrumbs for the birds, read out on the lawn, made some tea, waited for him to get back from work in his study. He was in a rare good mood, and joined her in the veranda after a workout in the gym. They talked like old friends, and laughed, and teased each other almost as in their early days. She hadn't felt that much joy in so long.

After their evening together, when they were in bed, she switched off the light, and took a look at his sleeping form. He was turned away from her, as usual. She placed a hand on his back; he didn't respond. She lay back, pulled up the covers and closed her eyes. The night lay deep and silent around them.

It started slowly.

She imagined a cluster of cells growing inside her.

Multiplying at an unusual rate. They wouldn't stop, now quickly spiralling out of control, gnawing away at their surroundings, turning upon themselves. It felt cosmic, like a connection to something deep in the universe that gave life and took it away.

It spread, like the veins of a city, seen from a flight at night.

Unstoppable, and eventually incurable.

The next morning, she awoke feeling better than ever before.

A MURDER IN THE WEDDING SEASON

Bulbul Sharma

The old house, perched on a steep hillside, groaned under the weight of two dozen relatives. Soni had stopped counting after the twentieth aunt arrived at the gate, sweaty and tired, asking for change for her rickshaw fare. Soni had hoped that the landslides caused by the recent rains would deter some of the relatives who lived further afield but not a single one had regretted the invitation to the wedding.

'Rai Bahadur Daulatji's granddaughter's wedding—no landslides can keep us away,' an uncle aged eighty-one had written, and arrived with his catheter in tow.

'Your late husband will be sad if we don't come. His soul will weep in sorrow when he looks down from heaven and sees we are not there,' said an aunt and landed up with her four unmarried daughters. Soni had planned for eight or ten people staying in her four-and-a-half bedroomed house in Shimla but now it seemed there were bodies everywhere.

Suitcases were piled high behind tables and every

available surface had a bedding roll spread out. The good thing was that no one needed looking after. Various aunts took charge of the kitchen while the uncles and nephews dealt with the tentwallah, keeping a watchful eye on the quality of crockery, the freshness of marigold garlands and the sturdiness of the hired aluminum chairs. Soni felt quite superfluous at times and ran away to hide in her bedroom, occupied, thankfully, only by her and her daughter Mita—the bride to be.

Soni had agreed somewhat reluctantly to this match. She was unhappy about her daughter marrying a boy from such an old-fashioned, wealthy family. Rohit was a well-mannered, intelligent boy and Soni liked him but she was nervous about Mita, so outspoken and wilful, fitting into a traditional joint family. Rohit's grandfather owned sugar mills and had vast acres of land in Uttar Pradesh where they lived in a huge mansion built in what Rohit jokingly called 'new feudal style'. Rohit's father was a well-known politician and his uncle was the local MLA.

'Rohit is a wonderful boy but his family—they are not like us,' Soni had said once to Mita but her daughter had replied, laughing, 'Ma, no one is like us. We are a unique family. Papa was a famous scientist but totally eccentric, you are unlike any other mother I know and Bobby is a child prodigy. Even our dogs are odd. Rohit's family is filthy rich but very ordinary and very boring.'

Soni looked at her late husband's photograph on

her bedside table and asked him once again, 'Do you approve? Is Mita doing the right thing?' His kind face looked at her, the black and white image as impassive as it had been in real life. His gentle, absent-minded eyes smiled at her. 'Do what you think is right, Soni,' she heard him say, in his 'don't bother me voice'.

~

'The knees are fine but my digestion is really bad,' said Banno Bua, rubbing her stomach gently to demonstrate. She was around fifty-five but behaved like a much older woman, keeping her head covered with her white lace-edged dupatta all the time. But her face was still beautiful and her large brown eyes darted about restlessly as if she was always looking for something she had lost. Banno Bua had a strong, melodious voice and was much in demand at weddings for her repertoire of old folk songs. Soni was not sure how the old lady was related to them but she liked her best amongst all the relatives who had come to attend Mita's wedding. Banno Bua helped with the chores quietly and never offered endless advice like the other aunts and uncles. She even helped Bobby with his school project quite happily.

Soni had once heard her sing a very naughty song but in a soft, mocking voice which others could not hear.

'I went to fetch water from the well, dear friend, but my brother-in-law caught me by the wrist...then by the elbow, then by the ankle...' she sang, laughing to herself, and suddenly Soni caught a glimpse of the girl she must once have been in that elderly woman's face.

'Don't tell anyone I sang this one,' she whispered to Soni, her eyes sparkling. Soni knew that Banno Bua had been widowed at a very young age and had probably had to learn to behave like all the older widows of the family. She must have trained herself to act like an elderly, sedate woman years ago, when she was still young. She must have erased her real self, bit by bit, to blend in with the family, till she forgot she was ever a carefree young woman.

Mita and Soni urged her one day to wear a coloured sari and a pair of pretty pearl earrings but Banno Bua shook her head. 'Never. Not safe for widows to look like parakeets. White protects us,' she said, giving them a blank, faraway look.

~

Now there were just three days left for the wedding and Soni finally discarded her anxiety and began to bask in the infectious, joyous spirit swirling around her old house. Every evening Banno Bua sang late into the night, charming everyone with her honeyed voice, and all the women gathered around her to form a chorus of discordant but happy voices. That evening she was singing a song about a docile new bride and her mean mother-in-law when she suddenly stopped.

'Who is that man, Soni, staring at us from the balcony?' she whispered, beating the dholki loudly to drown her voice.

'He claims he is a friend of my late father-in-law's and he's also Rohit's granduncle. He wants to stay with us instead of the hotel the boy's side had booked for him. "More fun with the girl's side", he said. I couldn't refuse, even though it meant giving him a whole room to himself, so inconvenient when we're so cramped for space,' Soni replied. 'He used to be an actor, they say. He is an MLA now.' For some reason she couldn't quite fathom, she did not like the look of this man who was smiling down at them, waving a red handkerchief. Gold rings studded with different-coloured stones flashed on each of his fat fingers. His face had a deep scar on one cheek and his dyed black hair had white patches, making him look like an old raccoon. He laughed and began swaying to the music, snapping his fingers, staring at the young girls.

Banno Bua finished her song abruptly and put the drum away despite everyone's protests. 'I am tired, I am going to bed,' she said and hurried away. Soni wondered what had upset her but then she forgot all about her. The singing went on for a long time and the children fell asleep on the carpet, clinging to their mothers' saris, and one very old uncle snored on the sofa, clutching his false teeth in his hands.

The singing finally ended and the guests drifted away, walking unsteadily with sleep-blind eyes to their various corners and crawled into their makeshift beds. Night crept into the old house and now shadows swayed languidly on the walls, as if still continuing the merry singing and dancing. A fine mist fell on the garden, touching the trees with damp, cold hands and the moon hid behind the mountains as if it was sulking. There was a strange, whining sound as the wind rattled the windows of the house and knocked on the doors, as if someone was trying to get in.

Soni opened her eyes with a start. Something had woken her up. Then she heard the noise again and jumped up from the bed. She went to the door and listened but she could not hear anything now. 'Must be the prawns you ate at dinner, giving you a nightmare. Go back to sleep, Ma,' mumbled Mita sleepily.

Soni could not go back to sleep so she got up and went down to the kitchen, tripping over someone sleeping on the floor in the corridor. Then she saw it was only a quilt and a discarded pillow. Someone was awake and walking around the house.

She wondered absent-mindedly who it was as she went into the kitchen to make herself a cup of tea. Then she went out into the verandah. The hills were still draped in a thick grey mist. It was almost dawn and the trees in the garden were touched by circles of grey-gold light. Later, Soni would remember that the birds were uncharacteristically quiet that dawn.

∼

It was the tentwallah's assistant who found the body when he was arranging the lights. He was perched on the top step of a ladder propped against the wall, draping the wires through the bars of a window in one of the upstairs bedrooms, and that is when he saw a body lying twisted at an odd angle on the carpet, next to the bed inside the room. The bed sheets were soaked in blood, and it looked as though the body had fallen off the bed. The tentwallah's assistant almost fell off the ladder as he turned around to shout to the boys working in the lawns below.

Then there was utter chaos.

The house trembled and shook as people ran around shouting and screaming. They tried to get into the room but it was locked from inside. Then one nephew climbed up the ladder and jumped in through the window. 'Oh my God! Dead! He is dead!' the nephew shouted to all the relatives gathered outside the door and they gave a collective cry of horror. The poor nephew barely managed to unbolt the door, before they all rushed in to get a look at the corpse.

Manmohanji had been dead for at least five hours, the doctor said, shaking his head as if he could not believe it. 'He was in good health for his age. If this terrible thing had not happened he could have lived till ninety,' he said, washing his hands.

The body was carried away for a post-mortem on a stretcher, draped in a white sheet. The relatives pushed each other to get a better look and an aunt fainted when she saw the bloodstains. The women wailed and the children hid behind the door in fear. They had forgotten to switch the music off and a melodious shehnai echoed all over the house as everyone talked in agitated, excited voices.

'He was stabbed by a thief who came to steal the wedding jewels.'

'No, no such a respectable man cannot be murdered. He had a heart attack, then fell down and cut his head.'

'This is a political murder. The opposition party must have sent an assassin.'

'Blood...so much blood for an old man!'

'He committed suicide. Cut his own throat!'

'That is impossible. You can cut someone else's throat but not your own. For suicide you have to cut your wrists and sit in a bathtub filled with water.'

'He died of food poisoning. Prawns are always dangerous.'

'What about the blood then?'

Everyone had an opinion. Even the children had got over their fears and were now running around looking for clues, led by Bobby.

The household was divided into two groups. The younger lot thought Manmohanji had been murdered and went around the house searching for clues along with the children, while the older uncles and aunts were certain he had died of a heart attack or food poisoning. They could not believe that a man from such a wealthy, important family could be murdered. Arguments and opinions filled the house. Soni's head was spinning and everything seemed like a bad dream. All she knew was that the wedding would now have to be postponed.

～

Police, press and more relatives arrived. 'Death due to unnatural causes,' said the police. Manmohanji had not died of a heart attack in his sleep as all the elder relatives had believed. He had been drugged and then his throat had been slit with a knife or some such sharp instrument. They had not found the murder weapon as yet.

'We told you so,' said the younger lot gleefully and threw themselves into a hunt for the knife.

The murderer had apparently mixed sleeping pills in the old man's bedtime Horlicks and then cut his throat. He (they all assumed it was a he) had cut the dead man's face with the knife for no reason at all.

The police called in everyone they thought was important for questioning one by one, which meant all the men in the house and the tentwallah's assistant. They left the women out since they did not want to upset them 'and in any case women never remember anything and make very unreliable witnesses,' said the young Inspector to Soni over his third cup of tea. His name was Ramesh Sen and he had been born in the same town that Rohit's family came from. 'A great, generous man he was—our Manmohanji. Just inaugurated our new police station building and now he is lying in the very same morgue. Life is very tricky,' he said, shaking his head.

The Inspector asked the servants a lot of questions and for two days Soni had to send for food from a hotel nearby because the cook was too upset to prepare any meals. Police suspected an old enmity. 'Some rival gang must have been jealous of his success, either from the acting world or someone from politics.

I suspect an actor, they have very fiery tempers and are very unpredictable,' said Inspector Sen. He sighed and then began telling Soni about his various health problems when he learnt that she was a Reiki teacher.

After three days of relentless questioning the police suddenly stopped. No one came to the house anymore and Soni learnt from a journalist friend that the police had been ordered to close the case. The Chief Minister was very annoyed with the bad publicity since the most shocking stories were appearing in the newspapers every day about Manmohanji's past life.

'Manmohan Thakur is now a liability to the party and his name should be erased without delay from public memory.' The Chief Minister wrote to the Inspector General of Police, and the IG ordered Inspector Sen to close the case at once. The file was stamped CLOSED and put in the old wooden cupboard in the back room of the Shimla police station along with other ancient unsolved cases.

The wedding was postponed. The mango leaf decorations wilted and were taken off, the flowers were removed although the bamboo poles around which they had been entwined and the wires for the lights still remained in place, giving the house a ghostly, ruined look. An uneasy quiet descended on the place as the relatives began to leave one by one.

'Dangerous lunatic in the house. Maybe our turn next,' they muttered.

'Bad omen, better cancel this rishta totally and find a new boy,' one aunt advised before leaving.

Soni did not know whether to be relieved or sad, though Mita seemed uperturbed. 'Rohit is not too upset about his granduncle. Apparently he was quite an evil fellow. When Rohit was a child he often punished him for no reason at all. He locked him up in the bathroom if he didn't finish his milk or forgot to brush his teeth. Even his parents were afraid of the old man. You know, Ma, he had many cases against him in their village in UP. Rohit feels someone from their village murdered him. Anyway, we can have a quiet wedding now after a few months. The old man did us a favour by popping off like this,' she said. Soni scolded Mita for speaking ill of the dead but had to admit to herself she felt relieved.

The house was now empty of all relatives. Only Banno Bua continued to stay on with them. She said nothing about leaving, just walked around the house mumbling under her breath. 'Poor old man. He seemed quite healthy to me. But you never know what is waiting for you around the corner. Fate always has a plan for everyone,' she said to Soni, her eyes shining in a slightly mad way.

Soni was worried about Banno Bua. Why had she not left with the other relatives? What was there for her to do in the house now? Bobby was certain she was mad. She kept asking Soni endless questions.

'Why did the police inspector leave? He should have spent more time here. How did the thief come into the room? The door was locked from inside. Must have been very clever, the murderer, don't you think? It takes a lot of strength to kill such a big man.'

One evening Soni had seen her go into the room where Manmohanji had died. She seemed to be humming to herself as she moved around the room, touching the bed, the chairs and the ornaments on the table. Soni had told the servants to lock the room after that.

'Mita, I am worried about her. Do you think this death has unhinged her mind?' asked Soni. Bobby, who was sitting with his laptop at the dining table, instantly downloaded a list of symptoms of insanity from Wikipedia, which he read out gleefully.

'Why should it make her go off the rails? She didn't even know the old man,' said Mita.

'She did ask me who he was. You know, that day when she was singing in the courtyard but then so did so many other relatives. Punit chacha even tried to borrow money from Manmohanji and was very angry when the old man refused. "Miser! Will he take his gold with him when he dies?" he had said to me, I remember. Poor man must be regretting it now,' Soni said.

'Why don't you talk to Banno Bua, Ma?' said Mita. 'You may not be able to cure her of her mental illness but you could at least calm her down a bit.'

'When is she leaving?' asked Rohit.

'I don't know. She has not said anything to me and I can't ask her "why are you still here?" That would be rude,' said Soni.

'Let her stay, Ma. I like her and she is harmless. All this murder business must have given her a thrill in her sad and empty life and she is making the most of it,' said Mita and Rohit agreed.

Soni put her book down and looked out into the garden from her chair in the verandah. There were potholes in the ground where they had stuck bamboo poles and all the plants in the flower beds were badly trampled. She sighed. The garden was her pride, and it would take her a while to get it back to its former glory. Suddenly Soni saw something glittering on one of the rocks near the rose bushes. She got up and walked down the verandah steps into the garden. The sunlight was falling at an angle, making the stone on the ring glitter. Where had she seen this ring before? Soni thought as she bent to pick it up.

She tried her best but could not remember. She walked thoughtfully back to the house, the ring in her hand. When she held it up to examine it more closely, she noticed there were dark brown spots on the gold. Could it be blood? Then she suddenly recalled Manmohanji's smiling face and the rings flashing on his fingers. She looked up and saw Banno Bua watching her from an upstairs window. She was in Manmohanji's room once more. The servants must have forgotten to lock the door that morning after they'd cleaned the room.

'Should we tell the police? I am sure it belonged to him,' Soni said to Mita, showing her the ring. She had placed it in a paper envelope since she did not want anyone else to touch it.

'Well, we should give it to them. It is evidence

after all, but I think they will just pocket it. Maybe we should just give it to Rohit's father. Let him decide what to do with it,' said Mita.

'The thief must have dropped it when he was escaping. It must have fallen out of the handkerchief,' said Banno's voice suddenly, giving Soni a start. She had not seen her come up behind her. The old woman moves so silently, it's creepy, thought Soni.

'Mita, there was no handkerchief. The ring was just lying there in the mud. Why did Banno Bua say that? How odd,' Soni mused as Banno Bua moved off and went out into the garden. They could see her plucking flowers for her pooja, singing softly to herself.

A strange thought was running through Soni's head as she shut her eyes and went back to that horrible night. She had been woken by someone groaning though she had never told the Inspector about it. Maybe she should have. Soni tried to think about that night. What had she done? Yes, she had gone downstairs to the kitchen. She had seen something on the kitchen table that had not seemed right. What was it? She had noticed it at that time and said to herself, 'How odd! That should not be there.'

But what was it? She just could not remember and felt irritated with herself.

The next day the mali found a red handkerchief in the rocky hollow below the pine tree at the far end of the garden. There was another ring in the muddy bundle. 'The police did not see this because it was under the fallen tree trunk. They were too lazy to search under the rocks,' said the mali proudly, handing over the red bundle to her. 'Do I get a reward? There must be a reward from the government,' he said, his eyes shining greedily. Soni gave him five hundred rupees though Mita said she should have given him more since he could have easily kept the gold ring.

Mita was obviously right because later she heard the mali mutter, 'Honesty never pays nowadays.'

How did Banno Bua know about the red handkerchief? Was she hiding something from them? The police had not questioned her at all though she always stood by the door when Inspector Sen was there. 'I must talk to her. Even if it's unpleasant. At any rate I must confront her soon and find out what her plans are,' said Soni to herself.

'We don't know anything about her,' Soni thought as she lay in bed that night. Something about Banno Bua bothered her now. She had seemed a simple, kind woman—a bit lonely—but now there was something furtive and secretive about her which she had not noticed before. What was going on in her mind?

Then Soni had an idea. She would go down to the kitchen, retracing her steps. Then she would remember what had been odd about the kitchen table that night. She often did that to jolt her memory into recalling things.

Soni opened the door silently and crept down the dark corridor. A faint flickering light shone through from the street light outside. Shimla still had the old lamps from British days that were struggling on bravely. Soni could not see anything in the kitchen so she made her way to the bedroom where Manmohanji had stayed. Where he had died. It had remained unoccupied since then because nobody wanted to sleep there but tonight the door was open. The servants must have forgotten to lock the door again. Soni put her hand out to switch on the light and suddenly a soft hand touched her fingers. Soni froze in terror. There was a figure draped in white behind the door. Soni opened her mouth to scream and then she heard the soft humming. It was Banno Bua.

'I have come to pick up my dupatta. I left it somewhere here,' she said. In a flash Soni remembered what it was that she had seen that night on the kitchen table. It was Banno Bua's white dupatta and it had red stains on it.

Soni opened her mouth to speak but Banno put her fingers on her lips. 'I know. You can see it all. I am a wicked woman and I have blood on my clothes. I will always have blood on my clothes,' she said, looking beyond into the dark garden.

~

She remembered his cold eyes, his smiling face looming over her. She remembered his laughter, her screams, the blood on her clothes, the gold rings on his fingers. 'You are a wicked girl, I knew it as soon as I set eyes on you. A shameless wicked girl!' he had said to her later as she lay sobbing on the floor. The shame burnt her entire being and she felt herself torn into shreds.

Her body twisted with pain as she curled herself tightly into a knot, like an animal about to die.

~

'Soni, beti, I wish I could have worn my red wedding sari for your daughter's wedding but I am a widow and it is not allowed,' Banno Bua whispered as she pulled her dupatta over her face. The she went and touched the pillow on the bed. Manmohanji's scarf was still lying there. Banno Bua twisted it in her hands.

'Did you know him, Banno Bua?' Soni asked softly though her heart was racing with fear. She must be careful not to say anything which would push this woman over the edge.

Banno Bua recited as though in her sleep, 'He came into my bedroom three days after my husband had died. "You must be lonely, my poor girl," he said, touching my face. I was fifteen years old and afraid of him. He was my father-in-law's rich cousin. 'I will take you away from here tonight. I will buy you pretty clothes. You don't have to wear white anymore,' he said to me. He tore my white sari off me that night, filled my body with shame. He put scars on me that I can never erase. I have waited for a long time to find him. I just cut his throat a little bit but he bled like a pig. Stupid old man!' She gave a laugh that was more like a sob. Then she threw the scarf out of the window. 'It is not far, look. I climbed up the ladder and jumped in through the window quite easily. I may look like an old woman to you but I am still quite strong. I can twist your neck for you. But you are a kind woman and I like you, Soni beti.'

Soni watched her silently not sure what to say and then Banno spoke again.'So now I can wear red at your daughter's wedding,' she said, laughing loudly and sobbing at the same time.

That night three days before the wedding, when the moon was hiding behind the mountains, the women found Banno asleep on the cold floor in the corridor covered with just a quilt and no mattress beneath her. 'Poor woman, she is used to sleeping on the floor,' they said as they retired to the room leading off from the corridor and settled themselves comfortably on the cots and beddings that had been laid out.

Banno Bua just lay quietly smiling to herself.

They never heard the door open. They never knew what took place in the room next to theirs.

He had not cried out when she entered his room. He was so pleased that she had come to see him though he was not sure who she was.

'You are a very pretty woman. Come, come sit by me. Tell me again, when did we meet?' he had asked. The stupid fool, too vain to wear his glasses! She had simpered coyly, slipping the pills into the glass of Horlicks on his bedside table. 'Drink it up while it's hot,' she cooed to him. 'Then we can talk .' She waited while he drank the Horlicks. Then, as his eyes began to glaze over, she had told him. She had touched the scar on his face that she had made with her nails that night long ago but by then he was already struggling to keep his eyes open. No, he had not cried out at all when she killed him, when she cut his face with her knife which was a shame because she would have liked to hear him cry out in pain like she had done so many years ago. It was she who had cried, a long moaning wail as though letting out all the grief she had held stored within her.

She shut her eyes and remembered his blood on her dupatta. Now they were even. It had taken many years but now they were even.

~

In the darkness, Soni saw Mita slip quietly into the room. She came and stood next to her. Banno sat on the bed and cried, her entire body shaking with each sob and in between her cries she tried to talk to them though they could not understand most of her broken words. It seemed as if she was talking in a strange language, using words they had never heard before. But they strung together the incoherent words edged with pain and understood what had happened one night many years ago.

Then Banno fell silent at last. The three women stood by the window and watched dawn break over the mountains and the sky paint itself a new colour once more. One by one the hill crows began to call in harsh notes and then the soothing song of a lone thrush began in the garden.

Mita held Banno Bua's hand and led her away from the window. 'We will find your dupatta. You go to sleep now and everything will be all right. There is nothing to be afraid of anymore. Ma and I will take care of you,' Mita said, speaking in a soft, soothing voice as if to a child.

Banno Bua nodded and smiled. She would wear her red wedding sari. It was in her suitcase along with the knife she always carried with her, hoping to meet him one day. She would keep the knife forever because she might meet him in another life. She would love to kill him once again.

AND THEN HE SAID

Paro Anand

And then he said, 'I could kill for you...'
Wet, wet. She was wet. Dripping her freshly showered body onto his, her lean, taut torso pressed up against his soft belly. Her long, thick, wet tresses dripping onto his own thinning hair, kissing him. Wetly. Her warm wet kiss was what he needed right now. And, as always, she knew what he wanted, needed. And she gave it to him, without him even asking. She always knew.

The way his wife never did. And now never would. They had stopped sleeping together a long time ago. They had continued to share a bed for a while, but then she found his snoring, his smell, his peeing a little bit on the floor on the way to the loo, intolerable. And so she had moved out of his room and right out of his heart. If she had ever been there. He thought about it one night, when he was desperately lonely. Had he ever loved his wife? Had he ever really made love to her, or had they just had sex? Had she ever enjoyed it? Had he? Probably not. It was more a dry and dusted act of procreation. Not much more. It was only later, much later, when Archi came into his life, that he knew what he'd been missing. Till then, he hadn't known there was much more to miss. It was more about needs than wants. But since Archi, ah! Since Archi...life had been worth living. Sex had been about more than bodily fluids and babies. It had become drive, pleasure, want, need, desperation, even.

~

She threw her wet towel at him as she got ready to leave. He was still wrapped in the hotel towelling robe, lying back, propped on the soft white pillows. He beckoned her to come back to bed. She laughed and shook her head. But he knew he could beg her back. He had an hour and a half before he had to get into his clothes and catch his flight. He lifted the covers, enticing her back. And she was undressing again. Feeling her body pressed against his, he wondered again as he sometimes did, what she liked about him. He knew what he liked about her. She was smart and sexy and always willing. And kind and caring to boot. But what was it that he offered her?

'What do I offer you?' he asked, cuddling her, burying his face in her silky hair, inhaling its freshly shampooed floral scent deeply.

'Hmmm?'

That was another thing he liked (loved?) about her. It was never a short, sharp *what?* Implying that he was talking rubbish as usual. It was a soft, cooing hmmm. A hum, to a tune, almost.

He repeated his question. 'I know what I like about you (like, not love. That was too big a word). But what do I offer you?'

She laughed, turning towards him, amusement sparkling in her honey-brown eyes.

'You? You offer me the best shampoo, the softest sheets and most of all, room service—with champagne, no less.'

'That's all?'

'Ummmm, no, there's also that big, squashy hug you offer me.' She giggled, rubbing his big, squashy belly, before kissing him on the nose and pulling away. Getting back into her clothes, deftly gathering her waist-length red-brown hair into a high knot which showed off her long neck.

'You'd better hurry too, if you want to catch your flight...' and she was gone.

He looked at his watch on the bedside table. It's okay, he thought, there's enough time. He was reluctant to leave the softness of the bed which still held the memory of her body. As did he. Ten more minutes, and then he'd race through his shower and head back home. Back to his family.

The familiar guilt pang shot through his spine. He enjoyed it in a perverse way. Like an addict who knows that the snort is going to get him in trouble, but he does it anyway.

The pang of guilt didn't trouble him too much. He would buy something nice for his wife. But for now, he put her firmly out of his mind and buried his head in the pillow which still held Archi's sweet smell of love and sweat. He held her wet towel against his skin. It still had her in it. He picked up her empty teacup from the night stand. He licked her lipstick off the rim. It tasted of her lips, her kisses. He kissed the rim, jealous that she had put her lips there. It was a poor substitute. He found himself wishing she didn't have to leave, even though he himself had to go. He shuddered with anticipation of the next time…and he remembered the first time.

~

The first time he'd met her. He'd gone to a conference, a genuine one that time. He needed to change his flight. He'd forgotten that his twelve-year-old had her arangetram, her very first public dance performance. He knew Anisha had been practising hard for it. He'd taken permission from his bosses to return home a day earlier. He'd gone to the conference travel desk to change his return flight. That's when he'd seen her. It wasn't love at first sight or anything like that. But he'd liked her smile and the way her two front teeth overlapped. It made her look childlike and sexy at the same time. Not that he was out there looking for sexy chicks. Of course not. He'd been married fifteen years and was a slightly paunchy, slightly balding forty-something then. Eight years later, he still wasn't looking for sexy chicks. Just the one.

Archana. Archi—without the 'e' at the end. Archana, travel diva, who kept her schedules dialled in with his own. There were a few times when he could travel, but she could not. He had suggested that she should give up her job. He would support her. But her 'naaahh' had been immediate. She was like that. Independent. A thought about her family flitted across his mind. Was there anyone else supporting her, father, husband, even? But he dismissed the thought with his own 'naaahh, of course not.'

Now there weren't that many conferences. But his wife didn't need to know that. He'd never meant to be unfaithful to her. He loved her in his own way. Well, at least he liked her. He wasn't big on this love thing. Always felt it was a bit overrated. Now he was not so sure.

The thing with his wife was that she was so immersed in her own things. Kitchen, home, family, her parents, his parents. And god. All good things. She had worked as an assistant editor for a family magazine. But when the children came and his parents and he himself had suggested she should give up her job and concentrate on being a mother, she had readily agreed. No 'naaahh' there.

He couldn't fault her for anything. Except being the biggest bore on earth. They had never had much in common and over the years, as they had first one child and then another, and mothering took up more and more of her time, they had grown apart as husband and wife. They'd never really been friends or partners in anything. The sex was all right, but it slowly exited their lives. So there was even less in common.

Not that it was any excuse. The affair just happened. He hated calling it an affair. It sounded so sordid and tacky and Archi was anything but that. She was classy in a way that he knew his wife would never be. Classy in a way he had never imagined he would get. He'd seen girls like her in shopping malls. But not in his wildest dreams or fantasies had he thought he could actually get lucky with one of them. She wore thigh-high boots while his wife wore chappals. Archi wore clingy jeggings. His wife wore loose, ill-fitting salwar kameezes which accentuated her large, loose stomach. Archi wore bras that were sexy even under her workout clothes. His wife's policy on bras seemed to be, 'the looser, the comfier, the better.'

Gravity did its cruel tricks on her. Archi defied gravity in every way possible. She literally flew through her exciting life. His wife was like a big, old comfortable tree rooted in her home.

Whereas Archi, well, did she have a home? Of course she did, everybody did. But he'd never thought to ask her about her home, her family. Her life outside of her job at the travel desk and in his hotel room bed. He didn't really want to, need to, know anything else.

It was in the taxi driving home from the airport that Archi's words came back to him. He felt a slight unease, like a burp stuck in the throat. She'd said she liked him because he afforded her the five-star life—champagne and soft sheets...was that all he was to her? Just a few hours of comfort in an otherwise drudgery-filled life? *Was* her life full of drudgery, or something else? Maybe he should ask her about her home? Did he really want to know more? Wasn't his life perfect enough? He shut his eyes to try and catch a nap and had a dream where his wife was a tree and Archi a high-flying bird. He awoke feeling relaxed and relieved. There was no need for probing questions, he decided.

And so his life swung along, between weighted gravitational pull and free flight. Everything was perfect. He bought two gifts every time, one to buy happiness, one to assuage guilt. He was a decent guy, a peaceable guy. Hardly ever fought with his wife, certainly never hit her, or his daughters. He wouldn't even step on a cockroach. He was a great father, a good, decent husband. Except for this one little thing. And she didn't know. It was all perfectly perfect. For not once did Archi ask him to leave his home and family, never once demanded marriage or some sort of commitment. Weeks flowed seamlessly into months.

Perfectly perfect, he repeated to himself as he disembarked from the taxi to enter the plush hotel. He was a regular. They knew him. They also probably knew what he was up to, but it was none of their business. Besides, it gave him a thrill. To be *that* man. The one who could be sleeping with a gorgeous young woman. Even though the bald patch was growing in tandem with the midriff.

They were eating in his room when she brought it up.

'How come we never meet at my place? You should see my home too, you know.'

'Why?' he laughed through the biryani and the slight stab of unease that went through him. 'Posh five-star not good enough for you?'

'No, it's not that, I love it, of course, just thought, I'd like it if you came to my house, too. Just for a change.'

'O-okay...next time.'

'Why next time?'

'Then? When? Today?'

'Why not now?'

She was determined. He didn't see why they needed to change what was perfectly perfect. He tried to change her mind. He tried to put it off to a next time. But she pouted and persuaded and that was that. There was nothing for it. So he agreed. Besides, she wouldn't let him make love to her until they reached her house.

'We'll do it there, it'll be exciting,' she nibbled into his ear. He didn't see the need to make this any more exciting than it already was. But she was young and the young needed change and excitement. And besides there was promise in her eyes. A wicked sparkle. And so he swallowed the little flutter of doubt and allowed himself to be led by her small soft hand.

His unease didn't let up as they took a bus. 'No, silly, not a taxi,' she laughed at him. He sat quietly in the bus, not enjoying the smells and feel of bodies pressed in close. He tried to imagine where she lived, but because he'd never asked Archi about herself, about the life she led outside of her time with him, he couldn't even begin to picture it. Where did she live? Did she have servants? Was there family? He shuddered momentarily. Was she taking him to introduce him to her family? The thought was terrifying. Was there a shift in their relationship? Was she going to start making uncomfortable demands on him? What on earth would he do? Break up with her? And do without all this? The thought of going back to his old boring life was too terrible to contemplate. No, he decided, he would try something else...his mind wandered off.

Yes, he thought with a start, he could take her to Las Vegas. What fun that would be. They could have one of those silly fake weddings there. How beautiful she'd look in a white gown. Yes, he'd get her one of those. They would stay at the Venetian. They would ride on a gondola. Oh, he was going to spare no expense for her. He could kill for her, then what was a little money? No one needed to know and Archi would be deliriously happy.

She almost had to pull him off the seat of the bus, so lost was he. 'You look so happy,' she giggled, giving his hand a squeeze. He looked around. The grey of the sky seemed to have leached onto the buildings. Into the lives being lived there, if you could call this living. Everything here smelled old and furry. As though the sun could not and would not shine onto this filth. It was like finding himself in an old black and white movie where Indian poverty was the theme. He had always hated dirt and squalor, he was fastidiously clean. Right now, he was living his worst nightmare. His sparkling hotel room with crisp white sheets and fluffy towels seemed worlds away.

She led him down a murky alleyway that stank of piss. Mangey mongrels with their ribs sticking out wagged their pathetic tails at them as they passed.

'That one's Lucy,' said Archi, taking a biscuit from her bag and stretching out her hand.

'Don't touch it,' he snapped. But she just squeezed his hand and gave him a smile, 'Oh, relax, I don't touch them, just feed the poor things. They're starving.'

Let them starve, we're better off without them… he thought, but he held his tongue. And his nose. They were at a doorway that led to a flight of stairs that smelt of something foul, and she had stopped. 'We're here.'

He couldn't help himself, 'Here…are you sure?'

She laughed out loud, that lovely laugh of hers, where she threw her head back and laughed out a real belly laugh. 'Of course I'm sure, what, you thought I don't know my own house?' But it was as if this doorway could not possibly hold something as bright as her laugh, something as wonderful as her.

'Err…no, I mean, are you sure we should be doing this? What's wrong with meeting in the hotel—it's… well…it's…'

'Clean?'

'Well, yeah, clean.'

'Tightass, you need to see how the rest of the world lives. And not be such a snob.'

'It's not a question of being a snob, it's just that I'm not sure why you need to do this.'

She was pouting and whining in a way that was not as sexy as when she did it in his hotel room. 'Oh, all right, if you really don't want to, then fine, be that way. I don't care. Let's go.'

She even took a few steps away from the door. She was genuinely angry, not playing anymore.

'Look, I'm sorry, I just, you know…come on, of course I want to see your house.'

And so they went up the stairs. Dark, dank and stinking. Something seemed to be crawling up with them, but maybe he was imagining it. But it felt as though a moist, furry, fungus-infested thing was creeping along beside him, step for step. He could almost hear it sniggering as his growing unease upped to pure fear.

She was jangling her keys in the keyhole. There was no light above the door. He took out his lighter and was just flicking it to help her when the door creaked open. Like in a ghost story, he thought. He almost reeled at the stench that met him. 'Geez…' he muttered. He could make out some bits of furniture strewn around carelessly. The light, such as it was, battled its way through a cloudy window.

To the front of the room stood a large sofa and table. The sofa was heaped with covers and clothes. The table was littered with bottles of medicines or something.

'Sorry, I'll open the window, it gets a bit smelly, sorry.'

But instead of going to the window, she turned to him, pressing up against him, her lips finding his mouth which was hanging open in shock rather than lust. 'I love you...' she murmured, 'I want you...'

Here, now? he thought.

'I need you to do something for me...' she whispered, gently biting his ear the way she knew turned him on. But he was not responding. He was taut with tension.

'You promised me something the other day, remember?' He didn't know what she was talking about.

'You said you could kill for me, remember?' Vaguely, he remembered, somewhere in their lovemaking, he may have said something absurd.

'You said you could kill for me and I need, I need for you to do it now.'

He didn't quite get what she was saying. Until the bite on his ear was not sexy, just painful.

'I need you to do it now,' she breathed.

'What?' he yelped like a kicked dog.

'You promised, you said you'd kill for me, I need you to do it. Look, he's asleep right now, he won't even put up a fight.'

He was sinking, the strength having left his legs, he tried to find the sofa so that he didn't collapse onto the floor. He sank onto the sofa but a moan escaped the heap of clothes. He shot right up to find himself held tightly by Archi.

'Archi, what the hell? Who's here?'

'My husband...'

'What? Your *what?*'

'Darling,' she whispered, though her voice was hard. He was trapped between her body and the sofa.

'Darling, he's ill, he's dying. Except, he isn't. He's been on his deathbed for years. He won't live and he won't die. So I want you to do it now. It will be easy, I promise.'

'Stop it, stop it. I need to leave. Now, right now.'

But he couldn't move. She was holding him tightly. And that's when he realised that there was someone else holding onto him. His legs were being held by whatever horror lay on the sofa.

'It will be easy, he's not going to fight you. You promised, you said you'd kill for me, do it now.'

He felt the cold, sharp blade pressing into his hands then.

'You promised...Do it.'

The blade pressed into his palm. He felt it break his skin.

'You or him, baby,' she said, her voice hard as shards, 'you or him. The choice is yours. There will be blood tonight...his. Or yours...'

He struggled. He pushed, hard. Adrenalin giving him strength. She fell. As he made a bid for the door, the hand from the sofa clung to him, he keeled over. He slashed out, freeing himself of those clutching hands. Winded, he struggled for the door on all fours. He pulled himself up and opened the door to freedom. He looked back one last time. She was still prone there on the floor.

He hurled himself down the stairs, heart pounding. He got to the grey street below and looked around, wondering which way to go. He was sweating into his eyes. As he lifted his hand to wipe his face, he saw it was covered in blood. Was he bleeding? He wiped his hand on his trouser. There was no wound.

Whose blood was it then? Had he...?

About the Authors

Sahitya Akademi award-winning writer **Paro Anand**, is best known for her fearless writing for young adults and children. She runs a programme, Literature in Action where she uses the safe space of story to explore difficult themes and issues with young people. She also writes for adults sometimes, especially when she is irritated with them. The story in this anthology is a great example. She was mad at her husband and wrote this story, leaving her beloved husband unscathed.

Venita Coelho worked in film and television for over a decade as writer-director-producer, before relocating to Goa. She is now the author of nine published books, including *Dead As A Dodo*, which won *The Hindu*/Good Reads award for best fiction for children 2016 and *Boy No. 32* which won the same award in 2019. Her other books include *Soap! Writing and Surviving Television in India, Monkey See Monkey Do* (nominated for *The Hindu*/Good Reads Award for the Best Fiction for Children 2018, and the Neev Literary Award 2018), and *The Washer of the Dead: A Collection of Ghost Stories*, which was recommended by Erica Jong as one of the ten best books on death and dying, and was long-listed for the Frank O'Connor award.

Uddipana Goswami is a poet and writer currently based at the University of Pensylvania in the US. Her published works include a poetry collection, *We Called the River Red: Poetry from a Violent Homeland* (2010) and an edited volume, *Indira Goswami: Passion and the Pain* (2012). She has also published an academic study, *Conflict and Reconciliation: The Politics of Ethnicity in Assam*, a collection of short stories, *No Ghosts in This City and Other Stories* and an anthology of folktales retold, *Where We Come From, Where We Go: Tales from the Seven Sisters.*

Manjula Padmanabhan is an author, playwright, artist and cartoonist. Her play *Harvest* won the 1997 Onassis Award for Theatre, in Greece. Her weekly comic strip *Sukiyaki* appears in *Business Line*, a Chennai-based financial newspaper. She writes a weekly column about her life in the US called *Here, There & Elsewhere* in 'BLink', the Saturday Magazine of *Business Line*. Her books include the novels *Escape* and *The Island of Lost Girls*, centered on gender conflict in a brutal future world.

Janice Pariat is the author of *Boats on Land: A Collection of Short Stories* and *Seahorse: A Novel*. She was awarded the Young Writer Award from the Sahitya Akademi and the Crossword Book Award for Fiction in 2013.

Her novella, *The Nine Chambered-Heart* was published by HarperCollins India (November 2017), HarperCollins UK (May 2018), and is being translated for publication into nine languages including Italian, Spanish, French, and German.

Currently, she lives in New Delhi with a cat of many names.

Mitra Phukan is a writer, translator and columnist who lives in Guwahati, Assam. Her published literary works include four children's books, a biography, two novels, *The Collector's Wife* and *A Monsoon of Music*, volumes of translations of other novels and a collection of fifty of her columns, 'Guwahati Gaze'. Her most recent works are a collection of her own short stories, *A Full Night's Thievery* (Speaking Tiger 2016), and another translated book, *Aghoni Bai and Other Stories* (2019). She writes extensively on Indian music as a reviewer and essayist. Her works have been translated into many languages, and several of her works are taught in colleges and universities. As a translator herself, she has put across the works of some of the best known writers of fiction in Asomiya into English. Her column 'All Things Considered' in *The Assam Tribune* is very widely read.

Pratyaksha writes and paints. She has published three books of stories, *Jungle ka Jadoo Til Til, Pahar Dopahar Thumri* and *Ek Din Marrakech*, a travel diary, *Taimur Tumhara Ghoda Kidhar Hai* and a novel, *Barishgar*, in Hindi.

Her other books include a collection of stories, *Rain Song* (2014) and a novella, *Meet me Tomorrow* (2016). A collection of erotic stories, *Mistress of Phoolpur*, is due to be published soon by Speaking Tiger.

She has won the Sonbhadra Katha Samman Award 2011, the Indo Norwegian prize for her story in 2013, the Krishna Baldev Vaid fellowship in 2013 and has been a fellow of the Sangam House Residency in May 2015 In 2018, she won the Hans Katha Samman for her story 'Barish ke Devta'.

She has attended the Bjornson International Literature festival, Norway, in 2014, and has also participated in the Kalam series of conversations held by the Prabha Khaitan Foundation in Patna, Raipur and Jaipur.

She lives in Gurgaon and is the General Manager, Finance, in Powergrid.

Bulbul Sharma is a painter and writer. Her works are in the collection of the National Gallery of Modern Art, Lalit Kala Akademi and Chandigarh Museum as well as in private collections in India, UK, USA, Japan, Canada and France. She has held solo exhibitions of her paintings in Mumbai, London and Delhi, and participated in group shows both in and outside India. She has written several books—these include *My Sainted Aunts, The Perfect Woman, Anger of Aubergines, Shaya Tales* and *Tailor of Giripul*. Her foray into crime fiction includes *Murder at the Happy Home for the Aged* (2018) and *Murder in Shimla,* due to be published by Speaking Tiger. Her books have been translated into Italian, French, German, Chinese, Spanish and Finnish.

www.ingramcontent.com/pod-product-compliance
Lightning Source LLC
Chambersburg PA
CBHW050338030726
47503CB00008B/2504